CENTER CITY CHURCHES

Ministry for the Third Millennium

CENTER CITY CHURCHES

The New Urban Frontier

EDITED BY
LYLE E. SCHALLER

ABINGDON PRESS / Nashville

CENTER CITY CHURCHES:

The New Urban Frontier

This book is printed on recycled, acid-free paper.

Library of Congress Cataloging-in-Publication Data

Center city churches : the new urban frontier \ [edited by] Lyle E. Schaller.
p. cm. — (Ministry for the third millenium series)
ISBN 0-687-04802-8 (alk. paper)
1. City churches—United States. 2. City missions—United States. 3. Evangelistic work. I. Schaller, Lyle E. II. Series.
BV637.C36 1993
250'.973'-091732—dc20 92-40681
CIP

94 95 96 97 98 99 00 01 02 — 10 9 8 7 6 5 4 3 2

MANUFACTURED IN THE UNITED STATES OF AMERICA

To
Gayle Carpenter,
Melea Edwards,
and
Gayla Oldham

CONTENTS

CONTRIBUTORS

Robert G. Borgwardt served as the Senior Pastor of Bethel Lutheran Church in downtown Madison, Wisconsin, from 1963 through March 1991. Earlier he had served churches in Wisconsin, Minnesota, and South Dakota.

Sang E. Chun, an ordained elder in The United Methodist Church, was born in South Korea and was educated at Yonsei University of Seoul and the Methodist Theological School in Ohio. He is Director of Evangelism Ministries for the General Board of Discipleship of The United Methodist Church.

Roger O. Douglas was called to serve as the Rector of St. Philip's in the Hills Episcopal Church in Tucson in 1977. Before that, he served as the Rector of St. Matthew's Episcopal Church in Wilton, Connecticut, for eleven years.

Robert Michael Franklin is Associate Professor of Ethics and Society and Director of the Program of Black Studies at the Candler School of Theology, Atlanta, Georgia.

James O. Gilliom has served as Senior Minister of Plymouth Congregational United Church of Christ, Des Moines, Iowa, since 1978. Earlier he had served churches in Indiana, Washington, and New Jersey.

Timothy Keller is the founding pastor of Redeemer Presbyterian Church in New York City. Before that he taught at Westminster Theological Seminary in Philadelphia.

Knute Larson has served since 1983 as the Senior Pastor of The Chapel in University Park in Akron, Ohio, where he majors on vision, pulpit, community involvement, and the Adult Bible Fellowships that have brought congregational life to this large downtown church.

Kevin E. Martin is Director of the Center for Leadership Training and Clergy Renewal of Episcopal Renewal Ministries in Evergreen, Colorado. He is an Episcopal priest and also serves as a parish consultant.

Norman Neaves is the founding pastor of the United Methodist Church of the Servant in Oklahoma City, Oklahoma. He is a graduate of the Divinity School of Duke University.

Randy Rowland is the Associate Pastor of Adult Ministries at the University Presbyterian Church in Seattle, Washington. He also owns a marketing consulting business in Seattle.

Lyle E. Schaller, a former city planner and municipal finance officer, is a United Methodist minister who joined the staff of Yokefellow Institute in 1971 as the Parish Consultant.

William M. Stark followed Raymond Swartzback as Senior Pastor of the First Presbyterian Church in Jamaica, New York. Previously he had served as the Senior Pastor of a large and growing racially integrated congregation in Kansas City.

Andrew J. White is the Hagan Professor of Practical Theology at the Lutheran Theological Seminary in Philadelphia. Before that, he served as the pastor of a Lutheran Parish in a racially changing suburb of Cleveland, Ohio.

Jeremiah A. Wright, Jr., is the Senior Pastor of Trinity United Church of Christ in Chicago, Illinois. He also leads a doctoral program along with Dr. Jawanza Kunjufu at United Theological Seminary in Dayton, Ohio, in "Afrocentric Pastoring and Preaching."

INTRODUCTION

In preparation for the first assembly of the World Council of Churches, to be held in Amsterdam in 1948, one document summarized the spread of Christianity during the previous one hundred years. It included this provocative statement: "There are three great areas of our world which the churches have not really penetrated. They are: Hinduism, Islam and the culture of modern cities."

Perhaps those words were written to provoke discussion, to motivate more aggressive evangelism efforts, or to stimulate action. Whatever the motivation, they represented a misreading of urban America.

Another contemporary misconception is that American Protestantism has abandoned the central cities as the churches have fled to the suburbs. While that does reflect what has happened in several of the older and long-established denominations, it is a misreading of contemporary reality.

While it is true that thousands of Anglo center-city congregations have dissolved, merged, or moved to the suburbs since 1948, that is only one part of the larger picture. It also is true that hundreds of other center-city congregations have shrunk drastically in size and have become dependent on denominational subsidies for their continued existence. But that, too, is only one slice of a larger pattern.

In several traditions, including the Evangelical Lutheran Church in America, the Christian Church (Disciples of Christ), The Presbyterian Church (U.S.A.), The Reformed Church in America, The Southern Baptist Churches in the U.S.A., the United Church of Christ, and The United Methodist Church, many, if not a majority, of today's largest congregations are to be found in central cities. While they include only one-sixth of the nation's population, large central cities account for twenty-six of the forty largest United Methodist congregations in the United States. According to the research of Dr. John H. Vaughan, who specializes in tracking the growth patterns of large Protestant churches, more than one-half of the forty largest Protestant congregations in the United States are to be found in large central cities as are more than one-half of the forty fastest growing Protestant churches in this nation. A disproportionately large number of the largest churches are to be found in the central city.

Despite the evidence that suggests the central city is a supportive environment for the large high-performance missionary church, the conventional wisdom has long insisted the opposite is true. This conventional wisdom can be traced back to the 1950s. Out of that came the widely shared conclusion of the 1960s that the traditional structures of congregational life created insurmountable obstacles to effective ministry in the city. A variety of alternatives was proposed. These ranged from a ministry of "a Christian presence" by a clergyperson who would be unencumbered by serving a parish to intensive training programs for the laity, who would be enabled to carry out a ministry in their workplace to urban training centers for the "retooling" of both the laity and the clergy to lay-led house churches to ecumenical action ministries apart from congregational life to a focus on community organization to campus ministries in urban universities that were not identified closely (except, perhaps, for financial support) with any worshiping community.

Overlapping that was the conviction shared by many mission executives and pastors that an effective ministry in the central city probably could not be expected to be financially self-supporting. Substantial financial aid would be required. It was widely assumed that one of the responsibilities of wealthy suburban congregations was to subsidize center-city churches.

Suburbia was seen as the new and challenging frontier after World War II. Most of the mainline Protestant denominations concentrated their resources on organizing new missions in suburban communities. One happy result was the creation of hundreds of large, vital, and strong suburban parishes.

In retrospect, however, it can be argued the most creative new frontier was back in the central cities. The competition for residents' attention, interest, participation, commitment, and support was and is far stiffer in the anonymity of the central city than in suburbia. One result was the widely publicized numerical decline of the majority of thousands of old center-city churches.

While it has received less publicity, far more important has been the emergence of hundreds of high-performance congregations on this new urban frontier. The purpose of this book is to lift up the ministry of these high-performance churches. Many of them are African-American congregations, another large group are predominantly Anglo, others are multicultural, multi-racial, and multi-ethnic congregations. A growing number reflect the immigration from the Pacific Rim, Africa, the Caribbean, Latin America, and India.

To gain a clearer understanding of the nature of these high-performance churches on this new urban frontier, it is useful to go back to a concept developed many decades ago by missionaries. They articulated the threefold goal of self-governing, self-propagating, and self-financing worshiping communities. If one accepts that as a definition of a missionary church in a hostile environment, these urban congregations can be described as missionary churches.

Those who feel *high performance* or *missionary church* are inappropriate terms may be more comfortable with two others. The first is *pilgrimage.* Every one of the fourteen congregations described here clearly is on a self-conscious pilgrimage. They do not attempt to recreate yesterday. They do not pray that next year will be a reincarnation of 1953. They earnestly seek to move in the direction God is calling them to go.

The other relevant word is *intentional.* They do not drift from crisis to crisis. Every one is on a pilgrimage marked by an intentional desire to discern and follow God's will. They do not expect their goals will come out of denominational headquarters.

The fourteen congregations that are described in this book were selected to illustrate what is happening in these missionary or high-performance churches on the new urban frontier. Before introducing them, two other points need to be explained.

First is the difference between *represent* and *illustrate.* The goal here is to illustrate several different types of strong, vital, and growing central-city churches. They were chosen to illustrate the range of what is happening. These fourteen congregations illustrate the presence in the central city of new, old, liberal, evangelical, charismatic, black, Pentecostal, middle-of-the-theological-road, conservative, liturgical, nonliturgical, large, very large, immigrant, ex-immigrant, Anglo, African-American, Asian-American, regional, community, racially integrated, independent, denominationally affiliated, low income, middle income, high income, working class, professional class, and socially inclusive churches. Obviously all of those selected illustrate at least three or four of those characteristics.

No effort was made, however, to draw a representative cross-section of center-city churches. The obvious omissions include the hundreds of small denominationally subsidized congregations, those that are growing older in the age of the members and smaller in numbers, and the thousands of small congregations led by a bi-vocational pastor. Likewise the hundreds of small, faithful, struggling, and obedient worshiping communities that are not interested in numerical growth are not represented in this volume.

The primary criterion in the selection process was to focus on what can be described as examples of high-performance, missionary churches in the central city. Hundreds of central-city churches can make a completely persuasive argument they should have been included if that was the focus. Why were they not included? The answer is simple: The purpose was to produce a book, not a catalog.

Second, a few readers may inquire about the distribution by denominational affiliation. That would be a relevant question if this were a book about churches in small town and rural America. The denominational label, however, is not a critical component of the identity of the large, growing, high-performance, strong, future-oriented, needs-driven, vital, missionary church in the large central city. The identity of these congregations is in (1) the quality of the ministry; (2) the personality of that long-tenured, visionary pastor; (3) the community outreach; (4) the members; (5) the preaching; (6) the music; (7) the weekday program; (8) an earned reputation; (9) the visibility, location, and accessibility of the real estate; and in many, but not all, cases (10) the radio or television ministry. The denominational affiliation ranks no higher than tenth or eleventh on the list of characteristics outsiders (and most members) use to define the identity of these high-performance churches.

Five groups of people still rank denominational affiliation high on the list of characteristics that define the identity of a Christian congregation. The first, of course, consists of denominational officials. The second is the parish clergy. The third group includes many, but not all, of the Americans born before 1930. The fourth group consists of adults who have lived all their lives in nonmetropolitan counties. The fifth is journalists.

Conspicuous by their absence are recent immigrants, retirees who crossed a state line to find a retirement home, American-born blacks, adults in their second or subsequent marriage, most adults born after World War II, Asian-Americans, refugees from a Roman Catholic heritage, Hispanic-Americans, never-married adults, those who place a high value on music as an essential component of corporate worship, and, most important of all for this discussion, residents of large central cities.

It may be true that, with the possible exceptions of the Roman Catholic Church and the Southern Baptist Convention, no one Christian religious tradition has been able to penetrate the culture of America's large central cities, but the fourteen churches selected for this volume demonstrate that the Christian churches are transforming the lives of tens of thousands of central-city residents. That is one explanation for describing these congregations as missionary churches.

One of the recurring themes in this collection of stories

about missionary churches is that they seek to listen to God and to be faithful to the call of the Lord. How does that happen in real life? That is the theme of the first chapter.

Where would it be most difficult, if not impossible, to launch a new mission that soon would be a self-governing, self-propagating, and self-supporting missionary church? One obvious nominee would be in mid-Manhattan in New York City during a major economic recession. The second chapter explains how that can be accomplished.

Whatever happened to the Jesus People who were so highly visible back in the late 1960s and early 1970s?[1] Is it possible for a group of Christians to replicate in a complex urban setting the model of the New Testament church described in Acts 4:32? What would a servant church look like in a neighborhood in Chicago, filled with the victims of urban poverty? Those and similar questions are answered in the third chapter.

Between 1963 and 1990 the population of Akron, Ohio, dropped by a fourth. Blue-collar employment dropped from 46 percent of all jobs in 1964 to 23 percent in 1990. Most of the large central-city churches saw their average attendance decline by 30 to 80 percent. One exception was The Chapel in University Park, where the worship attendance doubled to nearly 5,000 on the average Sunday morning. That is the story, to be found in chapter 4, of a congregation that decided to remain downtown rather than to relocate.

Back in 1932 a nine-year-old farm boy in Wisconsin began a lifelong hobby as a baseball fan. He suffered through forty years in the wilderness as his favorite team, the Philadelphia Athletics, moved, first to Kansas City and later to Oakland, before winning another pennant. Shibe Park, the old home of the Philadelphia Athletics, is now the new home for one of the largest Protestant congregations in North America. That transformation is the theme of chapter 5.

"We draw the circle to include people, not to define whom we exclude," explained a lay leader from Plymouth Church in Des Moines. Chapter 6 elaborates on that point to explain how large and liberal can be compatible in today's urban America.

One of the most significant characteristics of a missionary church is a clear identity. One example of when this can become a problem is when the immigrant congregation with a strong nationality and language identity seeks to reach and serve second and third generations who identify themselves as "Americans." A more sensitive and complex example is when a black congregation affiliated with a predominantly Anglo denomination seeks to reach and serve younger generations of African-Americans. That is the theme of the seventh chapter.

The next chapter recounts the pilgrimage of the oldest congregation in the book. It began as a Dutch Reformed parish in 1662. Today it is a model of a multi-cultural, multi-racial, and multi-ethnic ministry in the largest city in North America.

The Charismatic Renewal Movement has been one of the most powerful, and also one of the most widely misunderstood, factors in the renewal of the faith in the central city during the past quarter century. Chapter 9 tells the story of renewal in one central-city parish.

One of the big differences between the large central cities in the Northeast and Midwest and those in the Southwest is the capability of the city to grow in land area. Most of the older cities are ringed by incorporated suburban municipalities that prevent growth. Pittsburgh, Pennsylvania, for example, is locked in to an area of slightly over 55 square miles. By contrast, Oklahoma City is spread out over 600 square miles, and Tucson has grown from 80 square miles as recently as 1970 to 125 in 1986. Can the center-city church grow as the city grows? Two affirmative and highly creative responses to that question are found in chapters 10 and 11.

The past four decades have brought forth scores of experiments in campus ministries. In many, the frustrations and disappointments have exceeded the expectations. Experience suggests that many of the most effective ministries with both undergraduates and graduate students in the large urban universities is through networking. The parachurch organizations have demonstrated one model for creating and nurturing these informal networks. One of the most effective approaches, which builds in continuity with both the past and the future, is to begin with corporate worship. This has been a theme with several large regional churches. Chapter 12 describes a university-regional church on the West Coast, while the next chapter is about the evolution of an immigrant Norwegian parish into a large regional-university congregation in the Midwest.

The boats that brought the immigrants from Germany and Scandinavia have been replaced by the airplanes and ships that bring new generations from the Pacific Rim. Chapter 14 recounts the remarkable story of a relatively new immigrant church in a city that has become the new home for hundreds of thousands of immigrants from all over the world.

What can we learn from these high-performance missionary churches on the nation's new urban frontier? Each contributor has been asked to conclude by lifting up a few lessons from experience. In addition, the last chapter identifies thirty themes that surfaced repeatedly in working with large, growing, and vital center-city churches.

These thirty recurring themes help to explain the complexity and some of the challenges of ministry in the central city. They also can be used to create a conceptual framework for analyzing the role, identity, and ministry of your congregation.

Finally, these thirty themes are grist for the mill that grinds out a denominational strategy for ministry on this new urban frontier in the twenty-first century.

The dedication page represents (1) a tribute to that high level of competence necessary for effective ministry in the twenty-first century, (2) an expression of gratitude, and (3) a remembrance of the fact that this book was conceived on August 21, 1991, at an event in Colorado, sponsored by the Leadership Network.

Note

1. For another account of the Jesus People U.S.A., see the excellent essay by Timothy Jones, "Jesus People," *Christianity Today*, September 14, 1992, pp. 20-25. A sidebar by Julia Duin briefly describes what happened to five other intentional communities.

1.

"When God Says Stay, You Stay!"

Robert Michael Franklin

Driving along Atlanta's Interstate 20, the Reverend Cameron Madison Alexander surveyed his hometown's expanding skyline. The pastor of the historic Antioch Baptist Church, North, had a lot on his mind that day. Decisions had to be made about whether to move the congregation from its poor, crime-infested inner-city location on the edge of downtown to a pleasant suburban neighborhood where the congregation had purchased over forty acres of land. Suddenly, something extraordinary happened—God began to speak.

Alexander recalls, "God told me to pull over to the shoulder of the highway. Then, God said, 'Turn off the engine and engage the parking brake, we're going to be here a while.' " As if in the presence of a burning bush, the pastor obeyed and prepared to hear the words that would chart the direction of his ministry for subsequent years. The message was clear—God wanted him to build a great church in this inner-city neighborhood. Despite the results of several demographic studies commissioned by the congregation, all of which discouraged remaining, he embraced God's final instructions and promise. "Stay, and I will be with you." Smiling, Alexander admits that, as a child, he did not believe God spoke to people in this manner. Now, however, he reports, "We talk all the time; we talk that way."

Alexander shares in common much with another revered Atlanta preacher, the late Dr. Martin Luther King, Jr. Both individuals attended Atlanta's first black high school, Booker T. Washington High (1926), and the all male Morehouse College. Also, both are sons of prominent black Baptist pastors. While King was leading the movement in Alabama, Alexander was an activist and pastor in south Georgia. In 1969, one year after King's death, Alexander returned to Atlanta as senior pastor of Antioch.

Pastor Alexander is considered to be one of the best of Atlanta's treasury of pulpit virtuosi. A solid person of medium height, he flashes a broad, quick smile that softens the intensity in his eyes. In private, he speaks in a calm, deliberate manner, betraying a keen intellect in search of precise and pithy expressions. His measured tone is a marked contrast to the baritone trombone he becomes behind the pulpit. He is charismatic without a hint of flamboyance or self-protection.

Antioch Baptist Church, North

In 1877, African Americans in the South were adjusting to the federal government's withdrawal of support for their civil rights. Black institutions proliferated, especially churches and colleges. The Friendship Baptist Church, among Atlanta's oldest, became a "mother" congregation, spawning both new congregations and colleges (the all female Spelman College began in its basement in 1881). The eight or nine people who founded Antioch were from the Friendship congregation.

Known as the Bethesda Group, these people met in a butchershop for weeknight prayer meetings. Since Friendship Baptist was a mile away, they felt the need for a church in the immediate area. This nucleus correctly anticipated the astounding pace of urbanization of black people after the turn of the century. When the local and federal governments decided to build a massive public housing project in the fifth ward, Antioch was there across the street, ready to welcome the masses. In subsequent decades, the congregation welcomed numerous gifted pastors, but none with a tenure as long as Alexander's.

Antioch's Place in Atlanta

Atlanta is home to a treasury of significant black churches founded in the nineteenth century, including Friendship Baptist, First Congregational, Wheat Street Baptist, Big Bethel African Methodist Episcopal, and so on. The King family has made the Ebenezer Baptist Church the best known of them. However, only Antioch has constructed a massive new worship center in the middle of an impoverished community. Its location across the street from public housing is visually startling. But its presence there is also compelling. Poor people in the community trust Alexander and Antioch, and look to them for inspiration and physical support. By staying in the central city and investing its wealth and future there, Antioch affirms the value of people who feel rejected by the larger society. And this affirmation permits the congregation to challenge community residents to more responsible, productive living.

Alexander's long tenure at Antioch has earned him moral authority and political influence. Pastor and congregation are frequently highlighted in the city newspapers. Alexander's record of public-spirited ministry is impressive. He has served as Vice President of the National Baptist Convention, Inc., the largest black denomination in the world. Currently, he is the Georgia President of Jesse Jackson's Rainbow Coalition, and President of the State Baptist Convention. Antioch has invested wisely and owns expensive real estate throughout the city, including an old downtown hotel (The Walton), which the city government is renovating in order to accommodate homeless Atlantans. Antioch is quickly becoming Atlanta's most visible and socially involved congregation.

The Challenges of Exponential Growth

When Alexander arrived in 1969, Antioch boasted 638 members. In 1992, the membership roll contained 5,500 names. In 1990, a 5 million dollar Worship Center was dedicated. Members attribute much of this growth to Alexander's charismatic and prudent leadership. The congregation's greatest challenge was faced during the transition from a smaller, modest sanctuary to the gargantuan and lovely corner edifice. "Building the Church as we Build a Building," was the congregation's theme during the construction of the new facility.

Unusual for a church of its size, Antioch has no radio or television ministry. According to the Reverend Alexander, "word gets out by word of mouth." Although he speaks of being too busy building the church to be concerned with this common dimension of modern ministry, one has the sense that this pastor is working hard to preserve something sacred that might be imperiled if Antioch continues to expand exponentially. He often speaks of the intimacy people have experienced in the old building. The new facility represents both a threat to it and a vindication of its magnetic power for urban folk.

According to Dorcas Ford Doward, a member since 1983, dramatic changes accompanied the move to the large building across the street. She says, "We were afraid about losing that family feeling, and about becoming distant in the big building." Reflecting on the grief many people felt during the demolition of the old building, Mrs. Doward recalled the shock felt by many one Tuesday evening as people gathered for choir practice and other auxiliary meetings. Although they all knew the building would eventually be torn down, confronting it this way was painful. Someone in the crowd asked the pastor for permission to take a brick as a sacred reminder of the past. The idea caught on like wildfire. The next Sunday, Alexander invited the members to retrieve a brick. This gesture seemed to facilitate the process of terminating with the old and embracing the new space.

Jacquelyn Sorrel-Richardson, President of the Ministers' Wives Alliance, recalls the special feeling associated with "being crowded together in the old building, the old walls, creaking floors when you walked on them, hearing God's word and promises in a building that reminded you of days gone by." She says that for an upwardly mobile black population that enjoyed relatively comfortable homes from Monday to Saturday, the old building symbolized the latter days of sacrifice and struggle. The transition was difficult for everyone, she notes, and it was painful to suddenly be so spread out that one couldn't find one's friends.

This challenge reminds us of the spiritual and psychological significance of sacred space in the lives of parishioners. People must trust the space before they will allow themselves to be fully open to encountering the holy. Congregations that grow and build new structures must discover ways of expressing and integrating past, present, and future in their physical space.

A Liberating Congregational Culture

For Alexander, building the church from the inside out was the pastoral mandate. He faced the strenuous task of nurturing a liberating congregational culture before seeking to build a new structure. This entailed fortifying religious education ministries, more emotionally expressive music and preaching, and increased community ministries. The theological warrant for this ministry agenda is summarized in Antioch's formula: "Bible Based, Christ Centered, Holy-Spirit Led, and Mission Bound." The logic of this theology is evident during worship.

At Antioch, *worship* is a verb. Upon entering the sanctuary, one encounters a polished oak pulpit shaped to resemble an open Bible at the center of an expansive, brightly lit, and warm space. The open Bible pulpit invites interaction as one reflects on its contents before and after the work of the preacher. People gather long before formal worship in order to secure seats. This sense of anticipation is palpable throughout the service as the entire congregation interacts with the preacher, deacons, and choir. Drums and electronic instruments amplify the aural richness of the high-voltage worship. Colorfully clad choirs move to meticulously choreographed gospel rhythms. As hundreds of voices rise to God in praise, every worshiper has the liturgical license to stand, clap, weep, sing, pray, laugh, or sit in awe. During the "altar prayer," worshipers are invited to assemble at the front of the sanctuary, hold hands, confess their sins in prayer, and receive the absolution pronounced by the prayer leader. As people return to their seats, often with tears in their eyes, they testify that the "burdens of the heart have been rolled away." This sense of resolution of grief, guilt, pain, and despair prepares people to hear and participate in the preaching of God's Word. Thus effective music and prayer prepare people for transformative preaching.

Following this full sensory-engaging worship service, which runs almost three hours, people are invited to linger and have dinner in the fellowship hall. People who are lonely or live in stressful communities are in no hurry to return to them. The meal becomes a very important occasion for community building within the congregation. A state of the art walk-through cafeteria serves up healthy portions of soul food, which complements the nourishment just received upstairs. Like so many Southern congregations, at Antioch dining is sacramental. God's restorative powers are experienced through the therapy of fried chicken, collard greens, corn bread, hot biscuits, and peach cobbler, eaten in the company of people who are learning to love the Lord and one another.

As the congregation turns from evocative and interactive worship to its mission in the world, biblical guidance is provided by the cherished words of Jesus in Matthew 25:34-36. Although described as "The Six Ministries of Antioch," many more programs are clustered therein, including a Food Bank, Clothing Bank, Homeless Shelter, Prison Ministry (Project Redirection), Ministry to Persons Living with A.I.D.S., Substance Abuse, Narcotic Anonymous, and Senior Care.

I would suggest that Antioch's rich and robust congregational culture—evocative and sensory-engaging worship, triumphant singing, therapeutic prayer, imaginative preaching, and sacramental fellowship—makes possible, even necessary, a bold public ministry. Internal strength, joy, and hope spill over into a needy, unredeemed world.

Most of the new members flowing into Antioch are singles, between twenty-three and thirty-five years old. According to Doward, college students from nearby Clark-Atlanta University contribute to the seasonal swell of the membership. Surprisingly, the gender distribution is even. Alexander is proud to witness the reversal of the black male exodus from the churches. Like other interpreters of African-American culture, he is keenly aware that the future of black families depends on increasing the pool of marriageable men. He notes that the presence of men attracts other men, and it signifies that men at Antioch are respected and empowered. During worship, the visibility of men is as evident as the textual pulpit because men sit on the stairs leading up to it. It is extraordinary to see scores of young men sitting before the sacred book, hopeful symbols of morality, literacy, and responsibility. The pastor notes that this seating practice began as a necessity in the old building and became a tradition in the new one—another example of preserving the grass roots texture of Southern black congregational culture.

Traditionally, the black church has functioned as an extended family where pastors tend to be perceived as surrogate parents. Alexander is referred to as "daddy" by many of the younger members. Rather than discouraging this level of bonding, he permits it and seems to enjoy it. And he is anxious to see that everyone at Antioch feels connected with other people (a form of "fictive kinship"). According to a college student who recently joined the church, Alexander fosters a "family atmosphere" and "breaks the ice" during worship by instructing worshipers to touch, hug, talk to, and periodically make contact with at least five nearby strangers. He also likes Antioch because it reminds him of the church in which he was reared. Clearly, Antioch's continuity with the folk traditions and extended family ethos of early black churches has attracting power. Toward the end of nurturing this family loyalty, the church sponsors monthly men's and women's breakfasts, quarterly retreats, and regular joint activities.

Lessons and Challenges

After deciding to remain in the city, Antioch's challenge shifted to creating a structure that expressed its emerging self-understanding. It was poised to move into a league by itself—a wealthy, historic black congregation that was growing by leaps and bounds, committed to building a multi-million dollar facility on its original site.

After erecting the building, the people struggled to preserve the identity and character of Antioch. In order to preserve the warmth of the "old Antioch," church growth groups were developed. Today, groups are led by four current members who take responsibility for eight to twelve new members. For fourteen weeks, these Big Brothers and Sisters nurture then introduce new members to the larger congregation. Alexander reasons that new members will at least be able to recognize these familiar faces amid the sea of thousands.

In an effort to mitigate tensions between veteran members and new joiners, periodically the pastor ritually introduces the pioneers to new members. "New people need to know these are the bridges that brought us over." This inspired device incorporates old and new into an ongoing narrative of the congregation's experience and resourcefulness.

Alexander has advice for other pastors who are struggling with the decision to remain in or flee the city. They should remember that the church belongs to God and that God is coming back for it. Pastors should not assume ownership over God's prized possession. With this sense of stewardship, Alexander thinks that pastors should enjoy ministry, enjoy preaching, and learn to love the people.

Recall Alexander's highway talk with God. On the following Sunday, he announced that the congregation would remain and build in the present community as God had instructed him to do. He says that "you would have thought that I had hit the game-winning home run in a World Series. The people cheered and celebrated." He later discovered that many people wanted to move because they believed that Alexander wanted to do so. Paradoxically, Alexander sometimes wishes that he were still the pastor of the close-knit congregation that huddled together in the original building.

Perhaps, one of the most important lessons to be drawn from the Antioch experience is the reminder that congregations are called by God to care for the moral hygiene of the inner city. Ministry in pursuit of social justice will take many forms: legislative and political advocacy, direct charity, community organizing, and so on. Antioch is proof that some congregations are called to be in the fray of urban life, infusing it with the hope and power of the gospel. Antioch embodies the possibilities of inner-city Protestant congregations that embrace the vocation of being public churches.

2.

An Evangelical Mission in a Secular City

Timothy Keller

Why would anyone want to plant a new church in the largest city in the United States where only 7 percent of the residents are Protestant churchgoers?

Why would the small, Southern, suburban, theologically conservative Presbyterian Church in America (PCA) want to plant a new church in mid-Manhattan?

How did this new mission grow to a worship attendance of nearly a thousand in less than thirty months?

Why do the people keep coming back?

What does this experience teach us?

Knowledgeable insiders in New York pointed out the impossibility of doing any ministry in Manhattan without: (1) many connections, (2) much "street-wise" experience, and (3) a big endowment fund to keep the church going. "You'll never get the people you minister to to underwrite the huge costs of work here," said one rector. Several people told us that without all three of these things (and we had none of them), we should expect to stay small and struggling and to last about fifteen years, all with heavy subsidy from our denomination.

How Did It All Begin?

My involvement in this venture began back in 1987 when I received a request to plant a new mission in Manhattan. I was teaching pastoral theology at Westminster Seminary in Philadelphia, and although I turned down the call, I agreed to help research the field.

Over the next year I was oriented to New York City by Dr. Samuel Ling, a PCA pastor who had planted a Chinese church in Flushing, New York, in the early 1980s. Through weekly visits to do field research, I found myself becoming awed and stirred by the arrogance, fierce secularity, diversity, power, and spiritual barrenness of New York City in the late 1980s. In June 1988, after unsuccessful attempts to recruit other church planters, my wife, Kathy, and I committed our family to moving to New York to plant a church.

To gather a core group we decided to use a networking approach, rather than an advertising approach. The goal was to find a half-dozen key "gatherers," mature Christians who could bring new Christians to the church. New Christians were the real target for a core group, because (a) they had little church affiliation as of yet, and (b) they still had many strong relationships with non-Christians. Early on in our field research we met members of parachurch ministries who were seeing conversions among Manhattan professionals. We started our networking with them. Before moving to New York, regular commuting trips from Philadelphia uncovered four key couples who were "gatherer" types. All were deeply involved in ministry in the city, and only one couple was a member of another church in New York.

In February 1989, we began a prayer/vision-setting meeting on Sunday afternoons in the apartment of one of the couples. Gradually the group (attendance ranging from six to fifteen) developed an outline of the Manhattan professional culture.

1. The services should be warm but dignified and continuous with historic liturgical forms. The dignity and safety of liturgy and classical music appealed to the Manhattanite who frequented the theater, art galleries, and symphony halls. But on the other hand, the pastor leading the service needed to be extremely joyful and relaxed, needed to avoid all jargon, and had to explain everything ("confession of sin does not mean to grovel in guilt but to face our faults with honesty and hope").

2. The preaching had to be intelligent, bordering on the intellectual, but showing familiarity with urban life issues. Manhattanites are all experts in their fields, and they will only go to someone else they perceive as knowing far more than they about a subject. The preacher had to anticipate questions and objections to the evangelical message that would be raised by Jewish persons, socialists, Wall Street brokers, aspiring actors, gay rights activists, politically correct graduate students, and young second-generation Asian American professionals. If we always preached as if these kinds of people were present, they would come or be brought. Most Manhattanites had never met an evangelical with a college education. We decided to always present the classic Christian message in close connection with the issues we identified as "burning and relevant" to the average Manhattanite. Being Reformed in our doctrinal conviction and preaching was something we emphasized rather than diluted.

3. All outreach had to be through friendship networking. We did not do a shred of advertising. Since it was impossible to call on visiting Manhattanites in the traditional way (weeknight visits from strangers), all follow-up had to be by the friends who had brought them to church.

4. We emphasized a positive view of the city. We had to stress that our congregation was not an escape for people who hated the city, but an equipping center for people who wanted to meet a variety of needs in the city. We immediately began to stress volunteerism and service opportunities to help people in physical and spiritual need.

Implementing That Strategy

In April 1989, because we were still commuting from Philadelphia, we began a preliminary evening service on Sunday at 6:30 P.M. in a Seventh Day Adventist church, with a seating capacity of 400, at 111 E. 87th Street, just a few feet off Park Avenue in the Upper East Side. Fifty to seventy people began attending immediately, mostly newer Christians who did not have church membership in NYC. In turn, they began bringing nonbelieving friends who kept coming back. In late June 1989, Kathy and I and our three sons (ages five, nine, and eleven) moved to Manhattan.

On September 24, 1989, we added a morning service at the Adventist Church and decided, in the name of "options," to keep the evening service as well as a contemporary service. Approximately 90 people attended each service, and since 30 were attending twice, we already had a Sunday net attendance of 150. ("Net" means the attendance at all services minus those coming twice.) Our net attendance climbed to an average of 250 by the end of the year, with receipts of about $4,000 per week in giving. We were amazed by the number of people from nonchurched and non-Protestant backgrounds who returned every week and stayed after services, asking questions. In the spring of 1990 we added a 4:00 P.M. service (morning services can be too much for many Manhattanites who are up most of Saturday night). By June of 1990, we had a net attendance of 350. By fall 1990 we had taken in 100 members and had grown to 600 in attendance. We added a 10:00 A.M. service (along with our 11:30 A.M., 4:00 P.M., and 6:30 P.M. services). Giving had grown only moderately to about $5,500 per week.

The staff team developed gradually. In December 1989 we hired a demographics expert with a seminary education as administrative assistant. In March of 1990 we retained a Princeton Seminary graduate student as half-time assistant pastor in charge of education and music. (He became full-time ten months later.) In August of 1990 a family moved from Tenth Presbyterian in Philadelphia to Manhattan. He became associate pastor in charge of small groups and worship. We wanted all the staff to live in and be "energized" by Manhattan, not just tolerate it. All the staff were added while the mission church was still supported partially by the denomination.

In January 1991, the congregation decided to go off denominational financial support and to elect officers so as to be self-governing by June. A budget of $583,000 was approved. By late spring 200 members had been received, net attendance was running at 725, the giving was close to budget, and officers had been elected. On June 1, the officers were installed, and we became a self-governing church. By the end of 1991, we had 275 members and 950 were attending services. Typical figures for services were 200 at 10:00 A.M., 250 at 11:30 A.M., 150 at 4:30 P.M., and 450 at 6:30 P.M. Accounting for 100 people who come twice, we had a "net" figure of 950. In 1991, we also hired a secretary, a counselor, and a program administrator. The giving in 1991—our first year of self-support—was $694,000. The income met all expenses. The 1992 budget is just over $1,000,000, with approximately $140,000 earmarked for missions.

Who Comes?

One of the delights of the city is the diversity of humanity that clusters together in close quarters. In Redeemer we have had everyone from advertising executives, debutantes, editors, diplomats, Park Avenue matrons, Wall Street wheeler-dealers, Seventh Avenue fashion buyers, writers, lawyers, students, TV directors, critics, and successful artists to voodoo priestesses, high-priced prostitutes, pornographers, lifetime drug addicts, and the homeless. Kathy once watched with barely suppressed glee as one of Madonna's songwriters shared a pew with a Republican presidential speech writer! Scores of musicians, models, dancers, actors, and actresses, both making it and trying to make it, attend our services.

The testimonies of the converted include many that are not usually found in evangelical churches. One active man owns the most thriving bar in the neighborhood. We have card-carrying ACLU women lawyers who struggle very much with our church's position against the ordination of women, but they have been converted and become active anyway. One woman with strong objections to our position on women's ordination said, "It's odd, but I find women's opinions are more respected and their leadership more honored in Redeemer than in many mainline congregations I know." A smattering of "well known" personalities attend as well, though they tend to keep a low profile. There are managing directors of Wall Street firms, former longtime lesbians and gays, blue blood WASPS living on trust funds, Jewish men and women, former Buddhists, Muslims, and atheists.

The worshiping congregation is 85 percent single (though the membership is 70 percent single), and the married couples are mainly childless, so that out of 1,100 in attendance in spring 1992 there are only about 30 children on an average Sunday. The average age of the congregation is early thirties. Eighty-one percent of all members live in Manhattan, 91 percent from within the city limits. At one time in 1990 we discovered that 40 percent of everyone on our mailing list was within walking distance of the church. Vocationally, the church is 99 percent professional, rather equally dispersed between corporate and creative professionals. The worshiping congregation is 70 percent Anglo. The 20 percent ethnic is composed of 6 percent Chinese, 6 percent Hispanic, 5 percent Jewish, plus other members who are African American, Filipino, Japanese, Korean, Vietnamese, Lebanese, or Egyptian. Four-fifths of our Asian and Hispanic members are second-generation Americans. At least 12 percent of the members of this theologically conservative and evangelical congregation are known to the pastors to be homosexual. The actual proportion, of course, is probably much higher.

The consistent surprise of the ministry has been the large number of people attending without Catholic, Protestant, or evangelical backgrounds. We ask first-time visitors to sign cards, and 20-40 persons do so each week, but we are sure that represents no more than half the actual first-timers. Our observations indicate that 15-20 percent of the people present each Sunday are not Christians by their own conscious definition. Another 20-30 percent have been Christians for less than two years. One-third of our members join on first-time "profession of faith," and only one-third of the worshiping congregation has any previous evangelical background.

Why?

From a congregational perspective, five factors stand out in an explanation for our growth.

1. We present the evangelical message in an educated mode. Professionals are "experts" and want to receive high-quality teaching in Bible and theology. Many newcomers exclaim, "This is the first church I ever saw that really believes there are some answers to life questions, and yet doesn't tell people 'Don't question, just believe.' " This breaks the stereotypes most non-Christians hold of historical Reformed theology.

2. We worship in the vernacular. We consciously avoid both the coldness of traditional worship and the emotional manipulation of some charismatic services. We use classic Reformed worship forms (confession of sin, Scripture reading, expository preaching), but we make sure that the language is jargon-free and all concepts are explained. We aim in the music for quality and beauty rather than polish or hype, and we avoid all sentimentality like the plague. "The first time I came, I was amazed at how everyone was so emotionally and mentally engaged in the worship at every stage, yet there isn't the emotional excess that makes me uneasy."

3. We offer choices. Before the sanctuary was even half full, we began to break into two and three services. The services have different worship formats and music styles. The 11:30 A.M. service is liturgical with classical music, the 6:30 P.M. service is very informal with contemporary praise songs and jazz. The 10:00 A.M. service is liturgical with a mixture of historic and contemporary music. At the 4:00 P.M. service, the sermon is longer, and a question-answer time follows the service. Manhattanites love options and have responded well to the different ways to choose styles and schedules.

4. We encourage ministry entrepreneurs to begin "target ministries." These are lay-led programs that meet felt needs within the congregations and the community. At the beginning of 1992 these included a divorce recovery ministry; a ministry to people in job transition; three recovery groups, some run by a counselor, for people with various personal problems, including substance abuse and homosexuality; a support group for Redeemer members with AIDS and an outreach to the HIV-positive population; volunteers working with a local Habitat for Humanity chapter; a ministry providing tutoring; big brother-sister relationships; and tuition grants to single-parent families in a poor community in Upper Manhattan.

These ministries both win people into the church and give the newcomer the impression, "Here's a church where I can get help if I need it." Other ministries reach out to the needy and broken, and, though they are embryonic, Redeemer must be effective in such work if the gospel is to have any plausibility in this city where such needs are so great.

5. We build connections. Nearly two-thirds of all residents in the three zip code areas around us live alone. Loneliness is the greatest single need to address here. We have responded to this need through our cell group network. When we asked our associate pastor to begin a cell group program in the fall of 1990, he soon was able to form two dozen new groups.

The Denominational Role

Before discussing a few of the lessons we have learned, a word of appreciation must be offered for the contributions of the twenty-year-old denomination that includes only slightly over a thousand congregations. First, it was the determination and vision of Terry Gyger, the staff person for our domestic church planning program, to accept the responsibility for starting a new church in New York. Second, approximately $225,000 was raised to plant this new mission, thus enabling us to staff it for growth rather than survival. Third, and most important, we benefited from the prayers of many.

What Have We Learned?

1. You can reach the suburbs from the city better than you can reach the city from the suburbs. Some 5 percent of our members are young couples who have moved from Manhattan to the suburbs in the last twelve months and continue to be active in Redeemer. This is a trend that will continually lead to new churches around the suburban rim of New York City.

2. For sheer receptivity to the gospel, you can't beat the city. Suburban fears of inner cities have clouded our views of the ministry opportunities there. We are controlled by many myths: that the city is by nature irreligious, that stable ministries cannot grow there, that there is no one there but the poor. The city is actually a hotbed of spiritual opportunities. Wayne Meeks, in *The First Urban Christians,* shows why early Christian missionaries went to the city—because urban dwellers are more open to new messages than those in settled, smaller towns and villages. In short, urban dwellers are more open to new messages and are more open and able to making significant changes. Cities, therefore, are generally the most fertile evangelistic fields.

3. The real challenge of urban ministry is change. The real reason there are so many ministry failures in the city is not the lack of receptivity of urban people, but the breathtaking rapidity of change. Creativity and flexibility to meet new situations are critical. Churches who do not change their 1950s methods to minister to the 1990s may be hurt in the suburbs, but they are instantly destroyed in the city. The doors of opportunity open only briefly. To keep up with change, ministries must constantly do research.

4. New churches are still the best way to win new groups of people. The astonishing growth of Redeemer comes because it is a new church reaching a growing new population. Many denominations still have not gotten the point. New churches are better ways to reach new people than new programs in existing churches. New churches are led by the new people groups in a neighborhood, not by the older groups, and thus new churches empower people.

5. Prayer is always the irreplaceable foundation. That sounds like a cliche, and New Yorkers hate saccharine truisms, but we are forced by the facts to say this. When we received the 1988 "Love Gift" of our denominational women's organization, over 400 churches contributed and prayed for us. We received literally dozens of letters from big and little churches telling us we were being prayed for. I know of no single mission work that has ever had such visible prayer support—certainly in our church circles it was unprecedented. So why should we be surprised at the result?

We also have learned that leadership development is a never-ending challenge, that our longterm success will depend on our ability to help people on a religious pilgrimage become committed disciples, and that political stereotyping can undermine the ministry of any church. We also have learned that God blesses those who venture forth in God's name.

3.

An Intentional Community

Lyle E. Schaller

What model would you follow if you wanted to plant a new church in a poverty-stricken section of America's third largest city?

One alternative would be to turn to the New Testament and look at the model of an intentional Christian community described in Acts 4:32. Bring together a company of committed believers who would share everything in common.

What would be the central organizing principle in creating this intentional community? How does this sound? Our purpose is to live out our understanding of the full gospel: evangelizing the unsaved; nurturing, instructing, and counseling Christians according to sound biblical principles; and providing material aid, friendship, and other practical help to the poor as described in Matthew 25:34-40.

Who are the folks who might respond to that call to an evangelistic ministry that demands sacrifice and a seven-day-a-week expression of neighbor-centered love? One obvious possibility is some of the Jesus People, born in the decade following World War II, who were so highly visible as teenagers and young adults back in the late 1960s and early 1970s. A second possibility includes adults from earlier and later generations who share a similar worldview and value system.

How many people do you expect that call to ministry and sacrifice might attract? The answer in the Uptown Community on Chicago's north side is close to three hundred adults plus their children.

What would be the life expectancy of such a radical approach to urban ministry? How long would it last in our capitalistic culture? One answer is it is still too early to know. A better one is that it depends on how it is organized and on the leadership. Jesus People USA, a worshiping community in Chicago, is now in its twentieth year and continuing to attract believers.

What Is the Result?

When God mixed the answers to those five questions, He brought forth in Chicago a new ministry called Jesus People USA.

One component of this new urban ministry is an intentional community of approximately seventy-five married couples, sixty single men, and sixty single women who live a simple life-style together in a ten-story apartment building on Chicago's north side. Since anonymity is always a threat in such a huge community, they eat the evening meal in family groups of about thirty. They worship together on Sunday morning. They study, pray, and plan as one community. That building also houses a school for nursery through grade twelve that operates as a large Christian home school for 125 children.

A second component consists of the various businesses that are owned, operated, and staffed by the community. They represent the major source of income. These include a large roofing supplies firm, a carpentry team, painters, electricians, a recording studio, a video company, a magazine with a circulation of 60,000, Belly Acres T Shirts, a printing company, and a clothing and bookstore. Together they employ a hundred members of the community. Three common characteristics of these businesses are (1) the workers are partners, not employees; (b) each is organized around the exercise of one's creative skills; and (c) they offer attractive entry points for new members of the community.

A third component is music. The origins of this community trace back to the 1969–72 era with traveling Christian rock groups. The REZ (Resurrection) Band, founded in 1972, is an internationally known group that has given concerts on four continents. Other music groups include a hardcore punk band, an Irish-Celtic group, a rap group with dancers, and a gospel choir.

The big annual event under the music umbrella is the Cornerstone Festival, as 12,000 people—most fifteen to twenty-five years of age, but with a growing number of families—gather for four days over the Fourth of July weekend for teaching and music. This is now held on the 600-acre camp the community owns near Bushnell, southwest of Peoria, Illinois, and often includes fifty different music groups as well as nationally known teachers.

The fourth component is that amazing array of outreach ministries to those in need. These include feeding more than 200 dinner guests daily; Cornerstone Community Outreach, which offers long-term transitional housing for homeless women and children, including day care, counseling, classes in parenting, personal growth, and life skills;

Second Stage housing for twenty homeless families; housing and meals for ninety senior citizens on the top three floors of the Friendly Towers; the Uptown Crisis Pregnancy Center; employment opportunities for jobless men; chaplains at both the Cook County jail and a juvenile detention center; neighborhood Bible study programs; a research team on contemporary cults; and a variety of other caring ministries.

The fifth component reflects a growing trend among today's most innovative congregations. This is to accept the role of a teaching church. People from all over the world come to experience the life, ministry, and outreach of this intentional Christian community. Dozens of youth groups come for a day, a week, or longer to live and work in the inner city. The publishing, recording, and video ministries represent another expression of the teaching ministry. (For information on the July music festivals or for subscription rates to their monthly magazine, *Cornerstone,* write to Cornerstone Festival, 939 W. Wilson, Chicago, IL 60640. Tel. 312-989-2080. For scheduling a youth group to visit, write Youth Visitors, 920 W. Wilson St. Chicago, IL 60640.)

Jesus People USA is not the only intentional Christian community in Chicago nor in North America, but it is a challenging expression of the urban church of the twenty-first century.

What Is It?

The vision of ministry at Jesus People USA includes this statement: "We . . . have heard a call from God to reach Chicago's inner city and beyond with the gospel of Jesus Christ. [We are committed to] helping each member grow and mature in the Christian faith through an intensive environment of Christian fellowship, counseling, biblical teaching, and active involvement in vital inner city ministry."

First of all, this is a gospel-driven, evangelistic, high commitment, theologically conservative, mission-oriented, avowedly Trinitarian, interracial, and neighbor-centered congregation that places a high value on the family. One of the motivating forces behind this intentional Christian community is to create and sustain a healthy and supportive environment for the family.

This is the type of congregation that attracts a substantial proportion of newcomers from two slices of the population. One includes deeply committed Christians who are on a serious religious pilgrimage in their search for meaning in life. This group of intentional tent makers can provide a meaningful destination for these searchers and pilgrims. The second group consists of those who come for help and for healing. After having been helped and healed, some stay to minister with others.

How do the parents born back in the first four decades of the twentieth century respond when their adult child joins this first-century version of the Christian church? Some are puzzled, at least a few feel threatened, others become supportive, a very few become enthusiastic converts. Several prefer to change the subject when someone asks where their son or daughter goes to church.

Back in 1983 when the father of one of the leaders of Jesus People USA, and a very successful businessman, discovered he was terminally ill, he told his son, "You just keep doing what you're doing. What the rest of us have been doing doesn't make much sense." This father was deeply impressed by his son's happy marriage and wonderful family as well as by the son's strong sense of vocation.

While this was never a goal, and still is seen as a means-to-an-end, Jesus People USA today is a big property owner. In addition to that ten-story residential building, they own an office building, an apartment building for homeless families, a 600-acre camp, and a huge renovated warehouse that houses homeless women and children on the second floor, while the first floor serves as a place of worship for 500 people on Sunday morning and a dining room the rest of the week.

Why Has It Worked?

Scores of intentional Christian communities were founded back in the 1955–75 era. Most have disappeared, many without leaving a trace of their existence behind them. Why has this radical intentional community been among the few that have survived and attracted new members? No one reason is a sufficient explanation in itself. From this outsider's perspective, a dozen factors stand out.

The first and most influential is a profound desire by the members to discover and to follow God's personal call to them. This comes through most clearly as the leaders relate the story of their own individual pilgrimages. This openness to the leading of the Spirit also is a central theme in the expansion of their neighborhood and worldwide ministries and their businesses.

Second, this is a high commitment community. While no one is pressured by expectations laid on them by someone close, the leaders model high commitment. Living out the claims of the gospel in one's daily life requires a high level of Christian commitment!

From this outsider's perspective, but many of the members of this intentional community might not rank it this high, the third critical variable has been the determination to be a financially self-supporting community. A fundamental reason for the demise of many of the other intentional communities founded back in the 1955–75 era was their reliance on the financial self-support of parents, well wishers, churches, sympathizers, and friends. The passage of time causes many of the original supporters to disappear and for their potential replacements to question the merits of long-term subsidies.

Leaders at Jesus People USA estimate it is 95 percent self-supporting. The two big exceptions are (1) financial support from both public and private agencies, including other churches and individuals for the shelters and for feeding the hungry, and (2) loans from denominational sources for property acquisition. The loans, of course, are being repaid, but credit can be called outside assistance. The need to pay the bills from the income of the community has been a useful frame of reference for determining priorities.

An argument can be made that the fourth factor should be ranked higher. Unlike many other intentional communities throughout American history, this one is not organized around the personality of one magnetic leader. After a brief venture with that approach in 1972–74, this community chose the option of a leadership team.

This has many advantages. A team can keep the participants honest and accountable in a way that is impossible for the solo leader. Second, when that magnetic leader disappears, a huge vacuum is left. When one member of a team leaves, that person can be replaced because the continuity is in the team, not in one personality. Third, a team can mobilize a larger number of gifts and skills than can any one individual. Fourth, a team can model and practice peer accountability, while the individual leader reinforces the concept of a hierarchical model. This is especially important in (a) reaching the generations born after World War II and (b) creating and nurturing an intentional community in today's culture.

Overlapping this is a fifth factor. This is the affirmation by the leaders of the need for accountability. One expression of this is the 3,500-word covenant every prospective member is expected to study, understand, affirm, and sign. A second is the mutual accountability within that nine-pastor, interracial leadership team. A third is the weekly meeting of the leaders of the various businesses operated by the community. A fourth was an affirmation of the need to be related to Christ's universal church, which led to the decision to affiliate with the Evangelical Covenant Church—which has a college, a theological seminary, and a national headquarters nearby.

One of the most critical variables was the decision to concentrate on a servanthood ministry in this neighborhood. This neighbor-centered focus is both a reason for being and a cohesive force that strengthens this community of believers. It would have been easier to yield to the pleas to go out and plant Jesus People intentional communities in other parts of the world. This decision to serve where planted represents a crucial fork-in-the-road decision.

Another factor that is central to the life of the intentional community is the choice of a simple life-style.

An eighth clue to the effectiveness and longevity of this intentional community has been its policy to communicate the gospel in contemporary language. The most highly visible expressions of this are the music, the publications, records, videotapes, and concerts, but this also is a theme of the local servanthood ministries.

An openness to a new and different tomorrow also has been important. One example is the shift from emergency overnight housing for the homeless to long-term transitional housing. A second has been a shift in the attitude toward politics. Instead of remaining above and beyond the local political scene, the leaders reluctantly recognized that a servant ministry in Chicago today requires voter participation. That ten-story building at 920 West Wilson is now a polling place where nearby residents come to cast their votes. Political leaders also realize that well over three hundred registered voters live in that building and can vote simply by coming downstairs to the lobby!

One of the least publicized, but extremely important, characteristics of this intentional community is that it has two doors. Newcomers are welcomed if they want to come and try out this life-style. Those who find their personal and religious pilgrimage means they should depart are counseled, encouraged, and helped in making that transition. The covenant declares: "Ours is only one kind of expression of biblical Christianity among many in the worldwide body of Christ." For many who spent several earlier years on a religious pilgrimage, Jesus People USA has turned out to be their destination. For others, what appeared to be a destination became simply one more way station on a long journey.

When asked what was the biggest threat to the future of Jesus People USA, one of the pastors replied, "Materialism is always nipping at our heels. People do test the boundaries." One reason for the remarkable longevity has been the capability to identify and maintain those boundaries.

Finally, the ability to create, nurture, and sustain the extended families that welcome single adults clearly has been a factor in both the continuation and the numerical growth of what is a relatively very large intentional Christian community.

What will this community look like in 2014? That is a provocative, but relatively unimportant, question. Far more important is the call to be faithful and obedient to the call of the gospel today!

4.

THE CHAPEL IN AKRON

Knute Larson

My son attended The Chapel for a year before my daughter and I tried it. After only one week we knew this was where we wanted to be. I find that at The Chapel my spiritual needs are met and I am challenged to get involved. The people are very friendly!"

That brief paragraph by a blind mother summarizes the personality of this sixty-year-old center-city church.

We concentrate first on worship, the celebration of Christ and the Word, and the balanced personal application of God's Word to our lives. We seek to meet the spiritual needs of people, but we also challenge them to do more than watch. We encourage them to join the dreams—especially by getting in many "congregations" of the church.

From the outsider's perspective, eight other characteristics are lifted up repeatedly.

Downtown by Choice

First, we are a downtown church by our own choice. As far back as 1963, the limitations of our small site caused people to raise the possibility of relocation. Shortly after my arrival in late 1983, we created a Blue Ribbon Commission to examine our future. The first question we asked was "Should we stay or move?"

That committee of about twenty-five men and women of the church met frequently for six months to investigate that and other questions.

At the end of that time, ten recommendations were made to the staff and trustees:

1. Commit ourselves to our present, excellent location. Full steam ahead, here!
2. Engage a site planner to develop a master site plan related to buildings, traffic, and parking.
3. Continue study of the best use of facilities with multiple services Sunday mornings. Go to three services. We now offer both worship and study at all three periods.
4. Add new prime areas for Adult Bible Fellowships.
5. Expand and improve traffic flow, working with the site planner, administrator, and city.
6. Expand exterior lighting on all buildings and erect signs identifying The Chapel on Route 8, Buchtel, and Fir Hill.
7. Investigate the purchase of remaining adjacent properties for parking improvement.
8. Appoint a building committee to plan an addition for education, activities, fellowship, receptions, and gym.
9. Express appreciation to Akron University for the very positive "neighbor" relationship (we're right next door) and reaffirm our desire for cooperation and sharing.
10. Begin immediately building an infirmary-office-retreat center at Camp Carl.

Some of these recommendations are exact actions and others are simply expressions of gratitude or applause. We adopted all of them.

We is us. That is the beauty of ad hoc committees. We use people who really love and pray for the church and who do a ministry but then turn it over to the staff and trustees who must carry it out. The staff and trustees were represented on the ad hoc committee. As I studied with the committee, I came to the same conclusions. We decided to stay!

Why are we glad we stayed?

1. Our identification with the city. The Chapel loves Akron. It has a commitment to the city in prayer.

2. Influence in the city. Because of the size as well as its location, The Chapel is identified with the city, is respected by city leaders, and has some influence in terms of the mood or hopes of the city.

3. Connection with the university. The Chapel is located beside the University of Akron, a commuter school of over 28,000 students. While only about 4,000 live in dorms, this number includes a large contingent of international students whom the church has served for many years every Friday evening and as host families.

The university uses the main church parking lot Monday through Friday, and the church uses many of the university lots on Sundays. It is an arrangement honored by a handshake.

4. Accessibility. The church is downtown, at the center of the county, and at the crossroads of two main highways. Not only does that help on Sundays, but many people who are downtown for business or at the university stop by the church as well. It is very accessible to both Akron and suburban residents.

We Also Are a Regional Church

Suburbanites will come into the central city to worship, but few central city residents will venture out to the suburbs to go to church. That has been demonstrated all across the country. (See chapter 2.) Most of our people drive six to twelve miles.

One-half of our people live outside the city of Akron. Municipal boundaries divide. The regional church brings people together. Three out of ten new members are single adults.

We Are a Seven-Day-a-Week Church

Our location is ideal for our decision to become a seven-day-a-week program church. In 1991 we averaged 225 activities and events a week.

These activities range from the eight worship services every week (three main ones in the morning, one in the evening, Chinese church in the afternoon, a Vietnamese church, an international worship service in the evening) to support groups, small studies, and discipleship groups that meet during the week. Many groups meet at 6:30 or even 6:00 in the morning—usually five to ten in a group for study or support or accountability.

Our 8 percent annual rate of growth meant that in the fall of 1992 the Sunday morning schedule had to be expanded to four worship experiences with the first at 7:45 and the last at 11:45.

Children's ministries constitute one of our strengths, and youth outreach includes Wednesday meetings in nine locations so that the various high schools are served.

While the Wednesday program continues as it once was with a Concert of Prayer, we also offer electives for adults, choir and orchestra practice for over 300 people, and smaller support and study groups. The children's program on Wednesday also attracts many parents. Our weekday program provides scores of entry points for newcomers.

In the evening we duplicate many of our morning programs

for the benefit of women employed outside the home. Our gym is always a busy place.

One of the driving forces behind this extensive weekday program is our recognition that while God's grace is totally sufficient for justification and eternal life, human needs continue and must be dealt with in the local church. Most who get into ministry really touch other lives.

The heart of our congregational life is our Adult Bible Fellowships (ABF). These resemble expanded adult Sunday school classes. We call them congregations because of the emphasis on care, relationships, pastoral connection, fellowship, and outreach, as well as strong teaching with application. The Chapel has over thirty of these, ranging in size from fifteen to twenty to the average of fifty or sixty with several over one hundred. Our goal is to keep them at forty to fifty and then start new ones so that new people find their "community life" or "congregational life" in that ABF while still enjoying the benefits of the large worship and missions and outreach in the megachurch.

The church follows the pattern of "celebration, congregation, cell, college, and core." Most cell groups continued, in fact expanded, especially within the ABFs. Each pastor on staff is asked to lead discipleship and especially get men involved so that they can then train others, but most ABFs also offer small groups for either men or women or couples. Congregations are the best pool for cells.

We Do Utilize Television

Americans spend more time watching television than they devote to reading. So we produce and sponsor a one-minute television spot that is televised over an Akron station four or five times weekly. We target the unchurched, who will watch one minute but not sixty or thirty! These spots become an opening for people to talk about the church. Many of our people are asked about or comment on the spots to their friends.

These television spots are shown with the 6:00 evening news or with a national news program in the morning or a 10:00 evening program or on a Saturday afternoon sports program. Approximately one-third to one-half of our first-time visitors come in response to these television spots, which are produced and edited by volunteers from our congregation.

The television spots are mostly copy, but the scenery changes. I may be walking in the woods with a sweater and slacks or occasionally standing in the office wearing a suit and talking about a world issue. Another time I may be in a basketball outfit standing in the middle of the Cleveland Cavaliers' floor, talking about a Walter Mitty dream. Many times a spot is built around an adult object lesson that gets into the serious questions of life and Christ. All these spots are what might be called soft in approach, not pushy. "I urge you to consider how Jesus Christ could do this in your life" or "The choice is yours, but this is the way he said it" may be the concluding words.

Grace and Excellence

The fifth characteristic outsiders remark on is our emphasis on God's grace without legalistic barnacles and our pursuit of excellence. That covers everything from the design of the parking lot to our Adult Bible Fellowships, from our restrooms to our youth ministries, from worship to "The Minister's Agreement," which is signed by all leaders and teachers and calls for not only unity, but also an exemplary life-style and excellence in ministry. All our leaders try to announce and hold strongly to the fact that the number-one reason people come is the grace of God.

How Did It All Begin?

A sixth characteristic that interests many of our new members is our local heritage. Like hundreds of other central-city churches, The Chapel traces its roots back to one person and to a storefront. During the depths of the Great Depression in the winter of 1934, Carl Burnham gathered a group of people together in a storefront. Burnham was an evangelist with a special gift of being able to relate to people. Fifty people came that first Sunday. Two years later the congregation had grown to four hundred.

This rapid growth, due in part to Burnham's preaching, his evangelistic skills, and the congregation's ability to reach young married couples and youth, required a move to larger facilities. This move also produced the new name, The Chapel at Brown and Vine.

In 1949 a three-acre site in Fir Hill was purchased for $17,000. A new building that could seat 1,100 in the sanctuary was constructed at a cost of $375,000. This move led to another name change to The Chapel on Fir Hill. Many years later, when what had been a city university became a part of the state system, it expanded greatly and this area became known as University Park. So our name was changed to The Chapel in University Park.

When Carl Burnham died while undergoing open heart surgery in 1962, The Chapel averaged 1,900 at Sunday worship, 1,450 in Sunday school, and 900 on Sunday evening.

The founding pastor was succeeded by his son, David Burnham, also an excellent speaker, who had joined the staff six years earlier. During his twenty-year pastorate the congregation continued to grow in numbers, and a new sanctuary seating 2,400 was constructed. Home Bible study groups, youth ministry, and camping all grew during those two decades.

In mid-1982 David Burnham resigned to fill a pastorate in Boca Raton, Florida. During the fourteen-month vacancy period, three men led an exceptionally well-designed plan to search for the person who would become the third senior pastor in The Chapel's pilgrimage. I was called in 1983 from a fifteen-year pastorate in Ashland, Ohio.

The Succession Has Worked

When a stranger comes in to succeed the son who twenty years earlier had succeeded his father, most observers would predict this would turn out to be an unintentional interim pastorate lasting only a few years. The success instead has aroused the interest of many outsiders who are facing the issues of succession. When I arrived, I looked out every Sunday morning over a congregation that included the woman who was the widow of the founding pastor and the mother of my predecessor, hundreds of adults who had been won to Christ by one of my two predecessors, and many who wondered if I would change anything.

Why has it worked? We point to four critical factors:

1. Prayer. People really prayed for the transition to show that the church was not built around one person, to seek God's grace for the days ahead, and to continue their honor for the office of pastor.

2. Honor for that office. Because of the clear integrity and clean hearts of the previous senior pastors, there always has been a respect for the office of pastor. Others on staff also experience that respect.

3. Ministries. Many ministries and "congregations" within the church were added in the transition. It wasn't as if people just came and stared and wondered how the transition was going. Momentum and involvement helped smooth the way.

4. The Trustees and Search Committee. Their attitude from the beginning was that the office of pastor would be protected and they would not take over the duties that belonged to the pastorate.

Planting New Missions

The last characteristic outsiders inquire about is the planting of new missions. Denominationally affiliated congregations can afford the luxury of passing the responsibility for launching new missions to denominational agencies. As an independent church, we do not have that option.

During the past fifteen years The Chapel has planted five new congregations. In early 1992 they reported a combined worship attendance of approximately three thousand. We expect to plant another five new missions in the next ten years.

* * *

That is the story of a sixty-year-old congregation that has combined the roles of a downtown church, a university neighbor, and a regional congregation into a seven-day-a-week ministry that is eager to enter the twenty-first century.

5.

Reaching the Lost at Any Cost

Andrew J. White

In 1931, for the third consecutive year, Shibe Park in Philadelphia hosted the American League games in baseball's World Series. The Philadelphia Athletics, managed by the legendary Connie Mack, won a record 107 games that year, but lost the World Series to the St. Louis Cardinals in seven games. Twenty-three years later, after the 1954 season, the team moved to Kansas City, leaving behind the stadium that had been renamed in honor of Connie Mack.

Sixty-one years after the Athletics' last championship season in Philadelphia, that baseball stadium had been replaced by a magnificent $15 million structure that houses one of the three largest Protestant congregations in the northeastern region of the United States, the Deliverance Evangelistic Church.

* * *

Four years after the Philadelphia Athletics abandoned Connie Mack Stadium to move to Kansas City, Benjamin

Smith, Sr., was a metal impregnator for the Philadelphia Bronze and Brass Company. A few years earlier, following the death of his first wife, he had been depressed and despondent and suffering from severe headaches. Eventually he went to see a physician who, after extensive tests, told Smith that medical science could not help him. The physician's prescription was simple. "You need religion." That prescription led to the founding of the Deliverance Evangelistic Church in 1960.

* * *

Twenty-four years later, Pastor Smith approached a deeply committed member to take over the responsibility for developing the Hope Plaza Shopping Center on the site of the parking lot next to the old stadium. Smith said to this woman, "We will do this together." Her reply in accepting the challenge was to throw back at Smith his own principle. "No, pastor, you have asked me. Step back and let me do it. You have your own work to do." That was July of 1984.

Pastor Smith's idea was to have a self-sustaining village with jobs for the people, day-care services, a bank, and other services. In November 1984 this determined leader walked into a federal office in the city to get materials necessary for an Urban Development Action Grant. The federal official to whom she talked took on the airs of a Boston lawyer as she was told, "From your questions and responses to my questions, I am convinced that you cannot write this proposal adequately, and besides, you don't know anybody." To this she replied in typical Deliverance fashion, "I know *somebody*." Irritated, she walked out and one month later submitted the successful application.

The then representative of their congressional district, William Gray, called her personally with the news that she had won a grant of $1.15 million with the first ten years interest free, the second ten years at 3 percent, and the final ten years at 5 percent.

Next she went to a local bank, a fine old-line Philadelphia institution, and asked for a loan of $1.8 million more. She wanted a loan at 75 percent of the prime rate with a ceiling of 12 percent and no floor. The bank vice president to whom she was referred called her request preposterous, whereupon she asked him, "Do you mean that a black church of 8,000 members, many of whom have accounts in your bank in our neighborhood and with many relatives throughout the city, cannot get such a loan with your bank? Do you want to be one man standing up against 8,000 people and their friends and families?"

The bank official's reply was, "Are you threatening me?" "No," she said, "it's called leverage!" She got the loan on her terms.

The Philadelphia Authority for Industrial Development provided for a tax-free structure that also encouraged the bankers. An additional $250,000 came from the Philadelphia Industrial Development Corporation's mortgage program.

Next she turned to the problem of renting the stores in the shopping center. She worked out an arrangement whereby a grocery chain agreed to pay $175,000 per year plus a percentage over $12 million in sales in a 27,000-square foot supermarket. In the first year it averaged $500,000 per week in sales. That pattern has been followed in the the other fourteen stores in the plaza.

How did all of this come to pass?

* * *

Fifteen years after the Athletics' last season in Connie Mack Stadium, a dental technician by the name of Wesley

Pinnock left his native Jamaica to come to Philadelphia to improve his skills. He found a place to live in the home of a woman who was a member of Deliverance. On his first Sunday in Philadelphia she invited him to attend church with her. In 1971 he "accepted the Lord," became a member of Deliverance, and immediately enrolled in some Bible classes. At that time the Bible Institute did not exist.

Pinnock married in 1972 and thought of enrolling in Temple University to pursue training as a dentist. Instead, he found himself in the Ministerial Institute sponsored by Westminster Theological Seminary. When the Center for Urban Theological Studies came into being, with Westminster's help, and a pilot bachelor's degree program through Geneva College was established, he was one of the first students. He finished his bachelor's program in 1983, continued in an MA in religion program at Westminster, graduating in 1985 and later received the D.Min. degree from Westminster. Benjamin Smith was his strong supporter in the pursuit of this education.

In 1984 he became the director of the Deliverance Evangelistic Bible Institute, succeeding Dr. Joseph Ross, who currently is the public relations officer for Deliverance Church.

On January 17, 1992, Dr. Wesley Pinnock was named to be the Reverend Benjamin Smith's successor as senior minister of this huge urban church.

The Centrality of Prayer

How did Benjamin Smith, a blue-collar worker with only a modest education, build Deliverance Evangelistic Church?

Perhaps the best answer can be summarized in one word: *prayer.* Pastor Smith spends up to five hours a day in prayer. When urged "to get to work," his reply is that prayer is the work to which he is called. Everything that happens at Deliverance is centered on prayer. Pastor Smith never gives advice, but urges, "Let's pray about it." His prayers are from the Bible. His ministry is grounded in Scripture. He repeatedly refers, in prayer, in conversation, and in public utterances, to the Bible.

From a historical perspective the explanation must be expanded to a dozen words: *prayer, divine guidance, patience, faithfulness, obedience, evangelism, leadership, humility, vision,* and *simplicity.*

Prayer, however, is the central theme of this ministry, and that is how it all began.

How It All Began

Like scores of other very large churches oriented to a working-class constituency, Deliverance began with the vision of one person. Back in the 1950s Benjamin Smith was a member of the New Bethlehem Baptist Church in Philadelphia. He served as an usher, Bible school teacher, Sunday school superintendent, trustee, and chairman of the deacon board. His faithful service at New Bethlehem led finally to a decision to seek ordination in 1958.

"I tried all I knew how to avoid it. I said to my wife, 'Honey, I believe I am called to preach.' She said, 'Honey, everyone knows you're called to preach.' I was shocked. I thought for a while and said, 'I can't be a lukewarm, knock-kneed, weakling preacher. I have to have the power of God in my life. I see the need for revival, but I need God's power.' My wife said to me, 'It will come. How did you expect the Lord to manifest his power through you when you weren't listening to him?' That day I said yes to the Lord, and the burden lifted."

Following his ordination, Smith remained at New Bethlehem and at the Philadelphia Bronze and Brass Company. During lunch hour he would lead others in prayer and Bible study on the roof of the factory. He turned down promotions on the job, thinking that he would have less time for the Lord's work if he accepted. He is reported to have said, "With this job I had more church on the job than a lot of people have in church."

The Deliverance movement began to take form on New Year's Eve in 1959 when Pastor Smith, at home in prayer, sensed that the Lord was telling him to invite others. He got up from his knees and called several friends to join him and his family at their home. Many did not own a car, so he drove around the city picking them up.

By the end of the evening several were so excited about what had occurred that they began to talk of renting a store front so they could meet regularly. They had no plan to plant a church. They simply wanted the opportunity to follow their Pentecostal beliefs, to reach the lost, and to encourage one another. Most attended non-Pentecostal churches where their views were not supported.

During one of the Monday evening meetings, chosen so as not to interfere with other church obligations, the wife of a deacon in a local Baptist church received a prophecy from the Lord that challenged the group to "acknowledge God in all their ways and lead on." Smith's response to this was to suggest that the group form an evangelistic team and look for a place from which an outreach ministry could be launched. The deacon and his wife agreed, but the rest of those present did not, so the plan was postponed for the sake of harmony.

In June of 1960, again at a prayer meeting at the deacon's home, the decision was made to rent a facility at 25th and Jefferson Street where the group, now too large to meet in a home, could continue their Monday evening meetings. Soon the weekly crowd grew too large for the facility.

In the fall of 1960, Pastor Smith, now recognized by many as their pastor though he had not expected that to happen, asked whether the group was serious about starting a church. Ten persons said yes, and the next Sunday morning the Deliverance Evangelistic Church was begun.

From its inception, the group made it clear that they were not interested in drawing saved people from other churches. They were to grow by reaching the lost. One man who joined in those early days recalls that he had to get permission from the pastor of his own church before Deliverance would accept him.

After meeting for thirteen years in temporary quarters, the congregation moved to a 3,000-seat theater on North Broad Street. Before long the attendance at five worship services was averaging 6,000. Nineteen years later the new 10,000-seat sanctuary on the site of Connie Mack Stadium was dedicated.

Why Has It Grown?

At least four reasons can be identified to explain the phenomenal rate of numerical growth.

First, most of the new members have their initial contact with one of the outreach ministries. That list includes a drug task force, caring for the homeless, a prison ministry, street evangelism, college campus ministries, hospital and nursing home evangelism, and telephone evangelism. These are in addition to all the standard urban ministries.

Second, when recent members were interviewed, they emphasized the consistency of the gospel preaching. When asked, they could articulate the content of the sermons. Third, it is obvious to all that Pastor Smith lives the message he preaches. Fourth, as mentioned earlier, the foundation stone for Deliverance is prayer.

The Reverend William Moore of the Tenth Memorial Baptist Church, and chairman of the board of the Black Clergy Association of Philadelphia, calls Smith a humble man who is unassuming, committed, and visionary. "In particular, he is committed to prayer and a simple presentation of the gospel. He is a preacher without tricks," says Moore. "He has met the spiritual needs of the people without gimmicks so commonly used by others, and he has an exceptionally dedicated staff who share his vision."

Moore describes Smith as different from so many African American preachers whose ministries are personality centered. Smith's secrets, as Moore sees them, are that he trusts and delegates, he insists on outreach to all people, and there is a strong social component to his work as witnessed by the development of the Hope Plaza shopping center.

As it looks forward to the twenty-first century, this Pentecostal, Bible-centered, church includes a handful of Anglo members, a couple of physicians, many teachers, and a large number of low- to middle-income residents of the City of Brotherly Love.

A central part of the evangelistic emphasis is the altar call at every worship service. Individuals coming forward are invited to join the congregation if they are not members of other churches. If they wish to join, they are referred to Institute classes, like Discovering Your Faith I (understanding your Christian life role and systematic Bible study) and Discovering Your Faith II (transforming power of God through prayer, fasting, and God's Word). Many persons spend years in study within various programs (e.g., the counseling curriculum, the teaching curriculum, or the general theology program).

These courses can lead to a license to preach. While the paid staff at Deliverance includes only four full-time ordained ministers, another fifteen are ordained, but serve as volunteers. In addition, the congregation includes more than sixty licensed ministers. At least thirty-two of these licensed ministers have been commissioned to form affiliated congregations in Pennsylvania, Michigan, and Georgia.

What Next?

The new Deliverance Village includes the new church building, facilities for a Christian day school, and a child-care center. The vision for the twenty-first century includes a fully accredited black Christian college and a medical center.

When asked why the church has prospered, Pastor Smith says simply, "God made me aware of His plan to reach out for the lost. I began to seek His will and determined to yield at every point to His call. Jesus gets all the glory. The Holy Spirit is the executive director of the body of Christ. I am but an instrument, a channel of his grace."

* * *

That is the story of Deliverance. It is a credible story, verified by parishioners, fellow clergy, and public officials. If ever a church has grown because of simple preaching of the Bible and consistent demonstration of living the faith by the leadership, coupled with extremely focused evangelistic efforts by the people, then that is the secret of the Deliverance Evangelistic Church.

6.

Liberal and Growth Are Compatible!

James O. Gilliom

Conventional wisdom in recent years has declared that today's churches have two choices. They can be conservative and grow, or they can be liberal and decline. Plymouth is a testimony that liberalism and numerical growth are compatible.

Located in Des Moines, Iowa's largest city, site of the state capital, and a surprisingly robust center of business, communication, education, cultural and even international activity, Plymouth has stood for 135 years as a beacon of liberal Christianity—and it has grown to over a thousand at worship on an average Sunday morning.

A long-time member commented about how pleased he was that his church was becoming a "full-service church." With emphasis on clear identity of mission, quality programming, vigorous community service, effective worship, and faithful pastoral care, the members and staff of Plymouth still strive toward that goal. And, happily, recent membership growth has been one result.

A Long Tradition

Plymouth Church was "gathered" in 1857 when Des Moines was an emerging frontier town of 3,500 persons. The first minister was also principal of the public school, and ever since then the church has had an active relationship with community life. Another early minister helped form the Des Moines City Library. In 1893 the church financed the Sunbeam Rescue Mission to help "fallen girls, stranded working women, and unfortunate young men." One current old-timer tells his mother's story of how she "shopped" for churches in terms of their stand on women's right to vote. Plymouth met her liberal expectations.

In the early 1900s the Plymouth Playground Association built an indoor/outdoor playground for community children. The church helped build the Iowa Congregational Hospital and, during World War I, provided special programs and services for soldiers at Camp Dodge.

Its liberal theology made Plymouth a leader in interfaith and ecumenical ventures. During the 1930s its minister, along with a rabbi and a priest, toured the state to promote interfaith understanding.

Stoddard Lane, senior minister from 1929 to 1943, epitomized the liberal theology and social action of Plymouth's tradition. A pacifist even during World War II, a pioneer for interfaith relations and for racial justice, Stoddard Lane articulated that tradition:

> We impose no creeds. We do not insist on uniformity of theology or belief. We think there is room in a church for differences of opinion. We believe in the right of private judgment, and in the possibility of diversity in unity.
>
> Therefore we believe in the freedom of the pulpit, and of the pew. We take as our motto:

We agree to differ
We resolve to love
We unite to serve.

When we speak of Plymouth as a 'liberal' church, we mean that we try to keep an open mind toward the truth 'known or to be made known to us,' and we agree to disagree in the Christian spirit.

With all our differences, we are united in a common purpose to seek and practice the Christlike way of living for ourselves and for society.

How Are Things Going Today?

Plymouth currently has about 3,200 confirmed members, up from 2,500 in 1981, or an average net gain of 70 per year. During 1991, 175 new members were received and 78 were lost (36 by death, 21 by transfer, 21 by other reasons), for a net gain of 97.

Regular worship attendance at two Sunday morning services averages 1,004. In addition, approximately 600 children, youth, and adults are in Sunday education programs. Education opportunities also include weekday youth fellowship, athletics, Scouting, and adult classes, plus summertime and school vacation youth work trips and family camps.

Plymouth's music and fine arts program is extremely active, including visual arts, handbells, brass, and choirs. During 1991 we counted 479 persons in ten choirs. Five are children's choirs, averaging 35 each and starting with kindergarteners. A sixth- and seventh-grade choir has 40. The eighth through twelfth grade youth choir has become so large that it is divided into two sections of 70 and 75. And the same has happened with the adult choir, with a total of

125 who are divided different ways for different seasons and functions.

The children's and sixth- and seventh-grade choirs sing once a month in one of the worship services. Two Sundays a year the worship services are designed as contemporary musicals presented by the choirs. Each choir, in addition, plans some outreach, such as a performance at a retirement home.

The youth choirs provide the service choral music at the 9:00 A.M. Sunday worship. They also have their own outreach and fellowship activities, and each has its own out-of-state tour near year's end. That means 145 youth are spending a minimum of three and a half hours at their church each week, in addition to education participation, trips, fund-raisers, outreach projects, and other special services and concerts!

The adult choirs sing at the 11:00 A.M. services, present seasonal concerts, and go on tour. The two most recent tours were to Europe. On several occasions they have been invited to perform at American Choral Directors Association gatherings, and they have their own recordings. They, too, maintain a full program of fellowship and outreach.

A basic principle of all the choirs is that they are open to all who want to sing and accept the demands, and they are for volunteers. The only paid singers are the four section leaders for the adult choir.

The latest major addition to Plymouth's music and fine arts ministry has been the creation of the "Plymouth Fine Arts Series for the Community." With the threefold mission of bringing to the community excellence in the arts, consistent with the church's values, at prices affordable to as many as possible, the series has not only established Plymouth as being committed to quality community service, but has also provided Plymouth's choirs with extraordinary opportunities, on occasion, for their own participation. Most notable was a performance with the Dave Brubeck Quartet and guest soloists of his work "The Gates of Justice," based on words of the Old Testament and Martin Luther King, Jr. This was performed at the Des Moines Civic Center for an audience of 2,000.

A Family Life Committee plans several monthly special events for persons of all ages. These are as varied as a Halloween hayride, a January "beach party" at the Y, outdoor worship and a picnic at a park, attending an Iowa Cubs baseball game, and family camp. All are designed to offer easy entry for persons not involved in other, more structured and traditional, church activities.

The Cost of Growth

Plymouth's basic budget has increased from $233,252 in 1978 to $913,841 in 1991. Conference and national denominational support has increased from $49,095 to $101,793. In addition, however, an equal amount beyond the budgeted benevolences is given for other outreach causes, mostly local.

In 1978–79, $1.5 million was spent to add fellowship, adult education, music rehearsal, library, and office building space. In 1988–89, another $1.3 million was spent renovating the sanctuary, church school facilities, kitchen, gymnasium, and parking facilities. Improvements were also completed to make almost all the building accessible to those with physical disabilities, including an elevator built into the sanctuary chancel to provide access for choir members or worship leaders in wheelchairs. A twenty-passenger bus with a wheelchair lift was purchased in 1988.

Community Service Is Central

That century-old tradition of community service continues today. In 1968 a twelve-story retirement home for moderate-income elderly persons was built across the street from the church. In the 1970s church members helped develop the Homes of Oakridge low-income housing project, and the church continues to provide volunteer services. In 1989 a special gift of $36,681 from Plymouth launched a $1.5 million community campaign that resulted in a new activities center at the Homes of Oakridge. In the early 1980s we sponsored the resettlement of several Indo-Chinese refugee families. In 1990 we renovated an abandoned building into four spacious apartments for low-income families and gave the building to a local non-profit organization for management. Church members contributed $98,000, plus thousands of hours of labor by 175 volunteers. In 1991 a community playground adjacent to the building was completed by more Plymouth volunteers with an additional $11,000 in gifts. Food and money offerings are received one Sunday a month for the local food pantry, averaging several thousand food items and $10,000 annually. The Christian Social Action Board, through its Peace Committee, sponsors a monthly letter-writing campaign for Amnesty International. The Homeless Assistance Team gathers used furniture, which it stores in a rental unit until it is dispersed. Team members regularly assist in community feeding programs, being recognized by the Salvation Army in 1990 with its Group Service Award. During the coldest months, team members supervise overnight shelter at the church for those not accommodated by other community shelters, providing a hot meal, showers, cots, and breakfast. During the Persian Gulf War the Peace Committee led a series of ecumenical worship services that began at Plymouth and included Catholics, Jews, and Muslims. Special outreach offerings are received each Thanksgiving, Christmas, and Easter, usually for local community projects. These three offerings in 1991 totaled $28,186. Six boards and standing committees participate in a Plymouth-in-Action program that provides year-round opportunities for one-shot volunteer physical labor projects in the community.

The church building is heavily used by community service groups with no charge if endorsed by a church board. When the Raccoon River flooded in 1990, the Red Cross was given twenty-four-hour use of the fellowship hall and kitchen for emergency sleeping and feeding, with many church members volunteering their help. Our building became the city disaster headquarters for a month.

The ministers are encouraged to participate in community affairs. The Minister of Discipleship has chaired the United Way Allocations Committee. The Senior Minister has served on community boards, as president of the Ministerial Association and the Des Moines Area Religious Council and has had opinions published in *The Des Moines Register* on such public issues as teaching creationism in public schools, the Iowa rural crisis, abortion rights, Soviet-USA relations, condom advertising, televangelists, right-wing politics, the movie *The Last Temptation of Christ*,, and homosexuals. In the fall of 1990 *The Des Moines Register* featured Plymouth in a major week-long series on homosexuality. A few members left, but far more joined. The new-member class received in January 1991 was the largest in memory, fifty-five, (a class of twenty-six had been received in September), belying the assumption that heartland Iowans would not respond to a liberal presentation of the Christian gospel.

Why Do People Join?

A study was done of the two hundred adult members received (not including seventy Confirmation youth) from January 1990 to May 1991. Out of that total fifty came by transfer from other Des Moines churches, fifty had never joined any church, thirty-eight once belonged to some church but had become inactive, nineteen transferred from other UCC churches in Iowa and ten from out of state UCC churches. Thirty-three transferred from other denominations out of town. Nearly half (eighty-two) were couples with children, while twenty-two were couples without children at home. Another thirty were empty-nesters with grandchildren; forty-two were single people between ages thirty and sixty, many with children at home. Nine were in their teens or twenties. Only four were above sixty-five. Another significant statistic is that in 1978–79 there were thirty-seven funerals and twenty-seven baptisms. In 1990–91 there were thirty-five funerals and seventy-nine baptisms!

The study also included research on why people join Plymouth. The Minister of Membership concluded:

> People come to Plymouth because something good appears to be happening. The worship experience has integrity, and the church seems to be "on the move." It is not stagnating. It is aware of community needs and is involved in them. As one person said, "Plymouth doesn't just occupy a plot of ground, as did (in our opinion) the church from which we transferred."
>
> People come to enroll their children in our confirmation, music, educational, and service programs. They appreciate the high quality of these endeavors.
>
> People come because in seeking to activate a spiritual dimension in their lives, Plymouth meets their need, and in a positive way. They appreciate (although they may not always

agree with) the stands the ministers take. They appreciate the religious learning that is found. They appreciate the freedom of pulpit and pew.

They appreciate the compassion, the friendliness, the absence of judgmentalism, the absence of "clergy calling attention to themselves." These are the values and positive contributions to personal and community lives to which new members refer when asked, "Why did you want to join Plymouth Church?"

In a special celebration service for which members were invited to send in reasons they were thankful for Plymouth, these representative comments were heard:

"The music is so wonderful. The sermons are easy to understand, and we get something out of them."

"Relevant sermons, excellent teaching for children, critical involvement in community."

"I can be involved as I choose—no pressure—just opportunities. The pastors made hospital calls several times when our son was ill. My older son loves his church school. I also feel the openness and acceptance of all other people who attend—whatever attitudes, backgrounds."

"Because I am a lesbian, there are churches that have excluded me. For a long time I thought God was doing the excluding. Then I heard about Plymouth. When I came here, I understood that it was not God, it was people who didn't understand God's words. My partner and I have been welcomed with open arms, and I feel like I have found a place to belong and want to be."

"I can question my personal beliefs. No one at Plymouth demands that I believe as they do."

Growth Brings Special Challenges

1. Whereas largeness provides experiences and opportunities unavailable to the smaller church, it also has problems.

Individuals can get lost. At Plymouth a Membership Involvement Team interviews people about their interests when they join and then distributes the information. New members who do not already have friends in the church are assigned "shepherds." There is a six-month checkup on all new members and a regular five-year survey. Of the 127 adults who joined in 1986, the 1991 survey showed that 110 were still active, one died, eight transferred out of town, one transferred in town, four moved away and asked to be removed, and one moved in town and asked to be removed. To help the development of friendly relationships, a very popular breakfast is served each Sunday except during summer from 8:00 to 10:30 A.M. A "Nine to Dine" program forms small groups in which members host one another for meals in their homes during a year's time. More than 250 volunteer to participate. Each group in the church is urged to include relationship-building activities. Thirty deacons, equally men and women, help provide a friendly, welcoming, helping climate at all worship services.

Careful attention is given to the pastoral needs of the congregation. A team of lay visitors, under the direction of the Minister of Membership, makes regular calls on homebound persons, writing reports and meeting to share experiences. Another team of lay members divides Sunday altar flowers into smaller arrangements and delivers them to members in hospitals. The pastors meet semi-weekly to review pastoral needs and consult about the most effective ways to meet them. Hospitals are visited by the pastors three times a week, plus for emergencies. Pastors make in-home visits in preparation for baptisms and give high priority to pastoral needs and opportunities at the times of weddings and deaths. When counseling needs are beyond the training and skill levels of the pastors, persons are referred to the local ecumenical Pastoral Counseling Center for professional counseling, with Plymouth subsidizing the cost on a needs basis. It is not uncommon for professional counseling subsidies to run $500 per month. Extensive Women's Fellowship groups and a Men's Lunch Group offer many occasions for peer support, as do problem-related series of gatherings around common issues such as parenting, substance abuse, and the generation in the middle. Seven regular support groups are offered by the church and are listed in each worship bulletin and newsletter, with a number to call for information: Alzheimer's, Building Relationships, Divorce, Gay and Lesbian, LADOS (Life After Death of Spouse), Mastectomy, and Parents with Deaf Children.

2. As the church's activities have increased, so have space problems. Most children attend the 9:00 A.M. Sunday school, and that means we are crowded at that hour.

3. Because of the overcrowding of children's classes and the smaller pool of nonworking long-term volunteers for teaching, there is a problem of quality maintenance in the education program. An adequate number of volunteers are willing to help in the church school classes for a short term, but few will make a year-long, let alone longer, commitment as did previous generations. A proposal is currently developing to pay trained lead teachers who would be able to provide continuity and quality management for the sake of the children, at the same time enhancing the experience of the short-term volunteers.

4. Parking is a major problem because of the church's relatively small parking area and no opportunities for early expansion. Since we are committed to remain at this location, on Sundays we make use of the parking lots at nearby professional buildings. In the fall of 1991 the times of worship were changed, giving fifteen minutes more between services to

allow for "turnaround" time. A church bus picks up the elderly and people with handicapping conditions.

5. Finally, we face the problem of staff burnout. Ironically, the very synergism that develops when creative and highly motivated people work closely together is also the electricity that surges so strongly that circuits are blown. The expectations of the program staff at Plymouth are very high, both from the church members and from the staff members themselves. The pursuit of excellence can be both exhilarating and dangerous. The myth of Icarus, whose wings melted, sending him crashing into the sea because he insisted on flying too near the sun, sometimes seems eerily relevant. When staff energy unites in creative synergism, it is a joy to experience and blesses the whole church. When it is not united, it manifests itself in the destructive opposites of overwork, stress, depression, and negative relationships that hurt both the individuals and the church.

To prevent such burnout, the Plymouth program staff works very hard at communication—and communication means meetings. Normally, a good portion of each Monday is given to staff meetings. From 10:10 A.M. to 10:50 A.M. the program and secretarial staffs meet together for "treats," devotions, any issues of mutual concern, and calendar review. Until noon the music and ministerial staffs meet separately, each usually having lunch together. From 1:30 P.M. to about 3:00 P.M. the total program staff meet for evaluation of the past week, noting requests for newsletter space, sharing plans and issues for the next week (including the worship services), and bringing up any concerns for group consideration. About every six weeks, the Monday afternoon program staff meeting is skipped because of an all-day retreat at a staff member's home on Tuesday. Retreat days are informal, with time for relaxed conversation. The agenda, besides good food, includes devotions and longer range planning and concerns, as well as immediate subjects. The pastoral staff, in addition, meets on Thursday mornings to share pastoral information and clear final signals for Sunday worship.

Special attention is given to the continuing education of the staff. At least once a year an outside consultant is engaged to give leadership at an away-retreat setting. All staff members have completed the Myers-Briggs Type Indicator. On several occasions a trained interpreter has participated in a retreat in which personal types were shared and analyzed. Other such retreat subjects have included conflict management, working with volunteers, and ingredients of healthy leadership. Plymouth Church also provides its program staff with the funds and time for personal continuing education each year. And after five years of service each is eligible for a three-month sabbatical with full pay in addition to vacation time.

Additionally important in preventing staff burnout is the lay Personnel Committee of the church. Each program staff member meets along with the committee at least twice a year. It is through the committee's evaluation survey process that staff members receive feedback on their work from church members. It is also the opportunity for staff members to share their concerns about their jobs, salaries, staff relations, or any other matters. The Personnel Committee is vital in advising and counseling the Senior Minister toward the goal of having the most effective staff possible, serving the most faithful church possible.

What We Have Learned

Some concluding observations from Plymouth's experience would be that for a liberal, prophetic, socially active church to be vital it must:

1. Center on worship, with equal compassion for personal soul needs and clarity of social challenge.

2. Empower for service, with the offering of specific opportunities and the enabling means to fulfill them.

3. Support with education and care, that both commands the respect of the best minds and heals the most broken hearts.

4. Evaluate faithfulness and effectiveness regularly, with the criteria of both the biblical mandate and the human condition.

5. Believe in the need for change; it really is true that "time makes ancient good uncouth" (James Russell Lowell), that "the Lord has more truth and light yet to break forth" (John Robinson, pastor of the Pilgrims), and that God "is able to accomplish abundantly far more than all we can ask or imagine" (Eph. 3:20).

That is how we at Plymouth Church are preparing for the twenty-first century.

7.

Defining and Living Out Your Identity

Jeremiah A. Wright, Jr.

Trinity United Church of Christ is both unique and quite ordinary. As a new church started by the United Church of Christ in the early 1960s, Trinity was both unique and ordinary. It was an ordinary new church in that it followed the pattern of all mainline denominations' new church starts in the 1960s.

One aspect of the urban strategy of mainline denominations in the 1960s was to start new congregations in integrated or "upwardly mobile" single-family home neighborhoods where the residents were of the same socioeconomic stature. The residents were identified as prime candidates for membership in those congregations that sought "our kind of people." Trinity Church was ordinary in that it was "planted" in a middle-income, single-family home community. It also was designed to attract middle-income African-American professionals who desired an educated (meaning white) style of worship with a socially conscious focus on ministry.

Trinity is unique in that it did not maintain that suicidal stance and self-hating posture as so many other African-American churches did! This congregation was started on the first Sunday in December 1961. Ten years later the congregation changed radically the questions it was asking and the issues it started addressing. Instead of continuing to be a church for "our kind of people," the congregation changed and became a church for all kinds of people.

From European to African American

Instead of continuing to be a "middle-class" Negro church with European worship services, the congregation made a conscious decision to become a black church in the black community. That meant not only a change in worship style but also a change in focus, in mission, in ministry, in theology, in psychology, and in philosophy! That decision made Trinity Church both unique and quite ordinary.

It was unique in that it departed from the norm. It broke with the pattern of being an upwardly mobile, middle class congregation dedicated to the principles of self-preservation and self-perpetuation—that is, swelling its ranks by actively seeking out middle-income, middle-management educated blacks who were "a cut above" the rank and file or ordinary working class African Americans. The congregation broke with that pattern and self-consciously began to seek out all kinds of people. That made it unique as far as mainline denominations go and as far as many African-American, middle-income congregations go.

On the other hand, how that decision was reached made Trinity Church quite ordinary. The "ordinary" black church in large central cities is not made up of professionals only, middle-income families only, middle-management persons only; nor is it simply made up of persons who are educated homeowners a cut above the ordinary working-class person. The ordinary black church in major metropolitan areas is composed of well educated and uneducated members, professionally employed and unemployed members, members with good paying jobs and members with no jobs. The ordinary black church has within its ranks homeowners and apartment dwellers, Ph.D.s and high school dropouts, highly literate people and illiterate people, the "crème de la crème" and "salt of the earth" people!

The ordinary black church will have construction workers, computer operators, domestics, airline pilots, physicians, beauticians, garbage collectors, and college professors—all sitting on the same pew Sunday after Sunday. They will be singing in the same choir and serving on the same boards and committees week after week. Trinity's decision to become a black church in the black community made that congregation both unique and quite ordinary.

Prior to that decision, we actively sought out only certain kinds of people, but were not too successful. Since that decision, we are attracting new members from every walk of life, from every possible level of socioeconomic and educational status, and from every part of the city of Chicago and its surrounding suburbs. Our first sanctuary, for instance, was built four blocks from a low-income public housing project, but until the decision to change was made, no new members from that housing project were aggressively sought out. Any persons who lived in that project and wandered into our church were made to feel most unwelcome quite quickly.

Since the decision to change, however, we not only have over 500 members from several other low-income housing projects around the city, but we are now attracting low-income and wealthy members as well. We are now attracting young professionals from their mid-twenties to the mid-forties. We also are attracting those whom society considers the least, the last, the lowest, the lost, and the left out!

The change in worship style, incidentally, is what caused such a dramatic turnaround in the life and health of this congregation. Back when we fit the model of what mainline denominations said we should be, we went from zero members up to 300 in the mid-1960s, but we started dying in the late 1960s and were down to 87 members by the tenth anniversary of the church. It was then that the decision was made to change. As a result we now have 4,500 active members!

The worship style prior to the 1971 decision to change was a classic European (or New England Congregational) liturgical style with the added touch of Negro spirituals to show some inclusion of the Fisk Jubilee singers' tradition and the American Missionary Association's impact on the former African slaves through their massive educational effort. No displays of emotionalism were allowed. In the words of one of our former African-American National executives, "No niggerisms would be tolerated!" That approach to worship was one of the primary causes for the congregation's membership decline in the late 1960s and early 1970s, and the decision to change our style of worship was one of the primary causes for the meteoric growth that took place in the mid to late 1970s.

The New Identity

The current ministry of Trinity Church has three main foci that both best describe the congregation's unique role and explain why we attract so many new members. First, we place a strong emphasis on worship. Worship is no longer viewed as a period of mourning and solemnity, but is seen as a time of celebration, affirmation, joy, and praise.

We offer five worship opportunities every week at Trinity—three on Sunday and two on Wednesday. (The three on Sunday are all standing-room-only services.) Our worship experiences include elements from the African tradition, the European tradition, and the African-American tradition. We include the "old-time religion" devotional services and prayer meetings with testimonies, public prayer, and congregational singing. We also select songs from every imaginable quarter of the black experience, including spirituals, common meter, hymns, anthems, traditional gospel, and contemporary gospel.

Some songs are sung a cappella. Others use organ and piano accompaniment; and many use organ, piano, drums, synthesizer, bass guitar, lead guitar, congas, and saxophone accompaniment. We have five choirs. The Sanctuary choir (100 voices), the Women's Chorus (125 voices), the Men's Chorus (80 voices), the teenage choir, *Imani Ya Watume*[1] (60 voices), and the elementary school age choir, the Little Warriors for Christ (60 voices).

We also have a dance ministry consisting of children and teenagers. This has forty youngsters on its roster, and they dance regularly during the worship services on Sunday. The preaching ministry is central to the worship experiences. Preaching is not only a part of the three Sunday services, but it also is the centerpiece of the Wednesday noon and Wednesday evening worship services. It is this combination of factors—with heavy lay and congregational participation—that makes the worship experience one of the three main foci describing Trinity's unique role and its attracting so many new members.

The second factor that so many of our members say is unique is our heavy emphasis on Christian education from the Afrocentric perspective. Several of our new members have commented that ours is the first congregation to which they have belonged where they had so many opportunities to learn the Bible and their own history as African Americans. Many of them came out of churches where there were only one or two Bible classes. We at Trinity offer fifteen different classes a week every trimester. None of our members came from churches where anything was taught about the African heritage, history, or African origins of Judaism and Christianity.

Our Department of Christian Education oversees an extensive program that includes a wide variety of Bible courses, ranging from Paul Achtemeier's *Inspiration of Scripture,* through Latta Thomas's *Biblical Faith and the Black American,* up to Cain Felder's *Troubling Biblical Waters* and *Stony the Road We Trod*. In addition to our weekly adult Bible courses, we also offer eighteen weekly youth programs and ministries under the auspices of the Department of Christian Education. Those programs also have strong educational dimensions with a strong Afrocentric emphasis. Our youth programs include: (1) an after-school program in which African history and African-American culture are taught, (2) the Dance Ministry, where African and Caribbean dances are taught, (3) a reading tutorial program, (4) a math tutorial program, (5) the Rites of Passage programs for boys and girls (*Isuthu* for boys and *Intonjane* for girls[2]), (6) Saturday church school, which uses an African-centered curriculum for the children, (7) discipleship and confirmation classes, (8) martial arts classes, (9) Scouting programs, and (10) an athletic program. These options encourage youth to learn and participate in the life of the congregation, and they constitute another reason why so many parents are attracted to Trinity Church.

This emphasis on education also can be seen in several other areas of ministry. Each year on Thanksgiving Day, the congregation celebrates *Umoja Karamu* (Swahili for "the Feast of Unity") in which the pilgrimage of Africans living in the Diaspora is traced through ritual, song, dance, and symbolic food. Our entire congregation dresses up in traditional African garb, and thanksgiving is offered to God for the journey and for God's presence on the journey. In addition, every year for the past sixteen years, the congregation has celebrated *Kwanzaa* from December 26 through the Watch Meeting Service on December 31. We also offer learning opportunities concerning the *Nguzo Saba* (the seven principles) upon which the congregation places its emphasis in ministry throughout the year.

An all-church worship service takes place on the birthday of Martin Luther King, Jr., with the offering designated for a scholarship for one of our seminarians. The seminarians are required to write an essay (in competition with other seminarians) exemplifying how they are endeavoring to carry out a ministry that embodies Dr. King's vision of the beloved community. The emphasis on scholarship and education is not only for persons doing graduate study in the field of religion, but also reaches all the way down to elementary school. We now have more than fifteen of our graduates serving as parish pastors in other churches.

Our Scholarship and Education Committee sponsors an oratorical contest for all school-age children each year during African American History Month. The winners in each category are awarded with United States Savings Bonds. Every June on Scholarship Sunday, between $20,000 and $25,000 in scholarships is awarded to graduating high school seniors entering college, college students who compete through essays, and grammar school children who demonstrate marked improvement in math or reading scores throughout the academic year. This heavy emphasis on education and Christian education from the Afrocentric perspective is the second factor that makes our ministry unique.

A third distinctive facet of our total ministry is with our new members. As new members are taken into the church, they are taught in our new-member class what all of our ministries are doing. They are then asked to indicate as they sign their pledge cards (for a financial commitment) where they will work in the congregation.

What opportunities do we offer? Here are a few: (1) art, (2) Alcohol and Drug Recovery Ministry (which includes A.A., N.A., and "FREE 'N' ONE" programs), (3) athletics, (4) a counseling ministry, (5) a legal counseling ministry, (6) a ministry to and with disabled and physically challenged persons, (7) child care and Head Start, (8) Youth Church Ministry, (9) teaching in our church school or Bible study groups, (10) volunteering with one of the eighteen youth programs, (11) Long-Range Planning, (12) Single Adult Ministry, (13) Married Couples Ministry, (14) Allied Health Ministry, (15) Ministry with the Sick and Shut Ins, (16) AIDS Ministry, (17) Radio Broadcast Ministry, (18) Sisterhood, (19) Men's Ministry, and a (20) credit union. We expect our members to be engaged in ministry, and these options represent a few of those opportunities.

One of the ongoing obstacles we have to face is the question, What is the United Church of Christ? Most African-Americans have never heard of our denomination. The name alone puts up an unnecessary barrier for many people. They confuse us with the Church of Christ or with the Church of

God in Christ. Our lively worship and free expressions during the worship make many first-time visitors think we are a part of the Pentecostal family. (Some are relieved when they find out we aren't, and some are disappointed when they make that discovery!)

The literature provided by the denomination and the several classes on the African-American religious traditions have been the most effective means for overcoming this identity obstacle, but it keeps cropping up in almost every new-member class. The old stereotypes—like all Hispanics are Catholic and all blacks are either Baptist or Methodist—still live! It is hard to overcome stereotypes, and patient teaching seems to be the only option open to us in trying to destroy those stereotypes.

We now are one of the largest Protestant congregations in the city of Chicago. Two of the most important lessons we learned on our way to becoming the size we are now are the importance of being inclusive and the necessity for small fellowship groups and multiple small units for ministry. By inclusive, I mean we had to intentionally keep our church a church for "all kinds of people." Becoming a "silk stocking" church for the upwardly mobile drives away the unemployed, the underemployed, the blue-collar worker, and unskilled person. Focusing exclusively on the "working class" makes those who are privileged enough to have obtained an education feel like outsiders.

The need to design programs, ministries, cell groups, classes, boards, and committees and to create a sense of community that includes persons from both ends of the spectrum—and all those in between—is the most important lesson we have learned. That is the lesson that most urgently needs to be exported and utilized by other central-city churches. Not being afraid of people in the projects and not seeing them as "other" is crucial! Persons trapped in the inner cities must be seen as potential members—our members and our family—if a significant change is going to be made in their lives and in the life of the congregation attempting to incorporate them into that body of believers.

The necessity for smaller groups of ministry is what keeps a megachurch from becoming impersonal, cold, detached, or too big. One of the reasons new members are urged to become part of one of our smaller ministry groups is because this not only ties them into the body of believers in a significant and binding (and bonding) way, but it also is what makes church "happen" for them!

I would love to claim credit for having thought of that crucial idea for building a congregation, but the book of Acts already teaches us that this is how new members were assimilated following the day of Pentecost, when 3,000 new members were added to the rolls. Those 3,000 people "devoted themselves to the apostles' teaching and fellowship, to the breaking of bread and the prayers" (Acts 2:42). The reality of it is, however, that 3,000 people cannot attend Bible class together.

Three thousand people can neither eat together nor have prayer together. That happens in smaller units. In Acts 12 when Peter was miraculously released from prison, there was the church, "many were gathered together praying." Again, the reality is that 3,000 can't gather together in one house praying, but smaller units can. Smaller units not only can, they must if the church is to become the church and be the church for believers in our resurrected Lord!

That lesson must continually be relearned and utilized by all growing churches if we are to remain the church and not become just another civic group with a worthwhile social agenda!

Notes

1. *Imani Ya Watume* is Swahili for "Messengers of Faith," and it is precisely this African-centered focus that attracts so many members both young and old. The teenagers, their sponsors, and the pastor wear African garb on the Sundays they sing. The Sanctuary Choir also wears African garb on one Sunday of each month.

2. *Isuthu* and *Intonjane* are Swahili for "coming into manhood" and "coming into womanhood" respectively; not only are African words used as names for the programs, but African principles are used to teach values to the young people enrolled in the programs as well.

8.

A Multi-Cultural Church in a Multi-Cultural Community

William M. Stark, in consultation with Raymond H. Swartzback

The First Presbyterian Church in Jamaica, Queens, was founded in 1662 when the Dutch still governed New Amsterdam. The present sanctuary was constructed in 1813. One hundred and seven years later it was moved to the present location on 164th Street. Subsequently a huge church house—including a full-sized gymnasium, an auditorium, bowling alleys, and a variety of classrooms and meeting rooms—was constructed. During the 1940s and 1950s it housed a massive teaching ministry.

In 1892 Jamaica became a part of the city of New York. As the Borough of Queens grew, so did this congregation. The membership reached 985 in 1940 and peaked at 1,628 in 1951. The late 1950s and 1960s brought several proposals to sell and relocate the meeting place and rapid social and demographic change in the neighborhood as middle- and upper middle-income white families moved to what they perceived were safe communities. New residents in the community included large numbers of American-born blacks plus immigrants from the Caribbean Islands, Guyana, China, Africa, India, the Philippines, Latin America, and Puerto Rico. The active membership of First Presbyterian Church dropped to a hundred. Although the first black family had joined the church some years earlier, most members were middle-aged and older Anglos.

In the mid 1970s an exceptionally creative twenty-two month ministry by a wise, intentional interim pastor, Raymond F. Kent, placed the church in the position of seeking new pastoral leadership. Several longtime white "pillars of the church" and a handful of African-American members dreamed of a new era for this 300-year-old church. One of Kent's most significant contributions was to support, nurture, lead, and encourage the group of dedicated Christians determined to remain, and help transform what many perceived to be a dying church into a vital and relevant community-based congregation. The decision-making system was reduced to the Session plus two Task Forces, one on program and one on administration. This helped change the focus from survival to ministry. A young, enthusiastic, and gifted assistant pastor was called to revitalize the educational ministry. Worship became a celebration. As additional persons of color began to appear, they were warmly welcomed and invited to join. The average worship attendance moved back up to between 70 and 100.

The Pastor Search Committee worked with the New York City Presbytery in search of a permanent pastor who could help turn the dream of a vital ministry into reality. The search for a pastor brought several promising candidates who visited the area and evaluated the possibilities, but each left. In early 1975, Kent suggested the name of a pastor, Raymond H.

Swartzback, who had specialized in urban ministries for twenty years and who also had been on the staff of the Presbyterian Institute of Industrial Relations for the past twelve years. He was one of the best-known urban ministers, but he was completely satisfied with his present calling.

Eventually the Pastor Search Committee persuaded him to come to New York for an interview. He arrived without announcement early one day and spent that day getting acquainted with the community. The streets of this commercial area teemed with people. First, he walked one block from the church in each direction. Standing on a corner, apparently seeking directions, he stopped people and asked, "Pardon me, do you happen to know where I can find the First Presbyterian Church in Jamaica?" Three out of four persons he approached had never heard of the church, which was located just one block away. There was not one negative response to his question—just ignorance as to the church's location. If the church was that irrelevant to the life of the community, he thought, perhaps there was a chance to make an impact. Evidently the church had not turned people off. They were simply unaware of its existence.

He spent the rest of the morning and early afternoon walking the streets and striking up informal conversations with people, most of whom were very friendly. As the shops began to close, he boarded a bus filled with white persons headed for an outlying suburb. He sat next to a well-dressed man. As the bus passed a burned-out, graffiti-splashed building, he leaned toward the window whispering, "I'll bet you've seen some changes around here." It was like popping a cork. Attitudinal information flowed freely. The man owned a store on Jamaica Avenue. He was about to sell it because the neighborhood had changed. "They" had taken over. The man talked about politics, economics, and race, all the while castigating the various groups who now occupied the turf he once considered his own. The one-sided conversation was a sociologist's dream. It also was very sad.

When the bus reached its suburban destination, the pastor boarded a return bus to Jamaica. It was filled with persons of color: nannies, maids, hospital aides, and other workers. He sat next to a lady from India. She had received a Masters degree in English literature; she was working as a domestic. As the bus passed the same burned-out, graffiti-splashed building, he once again leaned over and whispered, "I bet you've seen some changes around here." She smiled and replied, "Much has changed since I moved here. The city has cut our garbage collection in half, the police are afraid to patrol, prices in the grocery stores have gone up, and the landlords must be hiding because we can never find them to make repairs. Everywhere we go we have to stand in line. All the powerful people who lived here when I first arrived have left. We don't understand it, for Jamaica was such a lovely community. They never took time to get to know us. Please don't make that mistake."

Swartzback met with the search committee the next day, and at the end of a four-hour interview, he and the committee members agreed the next step was not to talk about salary, housing, and other components of a compensation package, but rather to agree on a design for ministry. Three weeks later the candidate returned with a design that opened with this challenge: "For this church to survive it will take at least five years of hard work by the pastors and the congregation to establish a trust relationship with the community. Do you think the congregation will be that patient?"

The rest of the design called for affirming the role of the First Presbyterian Church in Jamaica as a "multi-ethnic, multiracial, multi-cultural congregation," focused on the immediate community. The committee accepted the challenge, endorsed the goals, and recommended the congregation call Raymond H. Swartzback as pastor. They did. He accepted. He stayed until he retired thirteen years later.

Two African-American women joined the staff; one was called as the new associate minister and the other as program coordinator. The church became a community-oriented, seven-day-a-week, year-round program church. During his service as pastor, Swartzback averaged 50 pastoral calls a month. By 1987 the active membership had climbed to 424, the number of members under age 40 had quadrupled from 44 to 185. Average attendance at Sunday morning worship was 240. The membership was approximately 40 percent American-born African Americans, 10 percent white, 40 percent Caribbean-born, and 10 percent other nationalities and ethnic groups. Nearly three dozen nationalities were represented in the membership.

What Happened Next?

What happens when that ideal match between a pastor and a parish comes to an end after a long and exciting pastorate? During the two-year period without a permanent pastor, the average worship attendance dropped by one third and the church school attendance plummeted. The heroic efforts of a small number of volunteers plus the part-time staff and a different preacher every Sunday, were not sufficient. Twice the search committee members were convinced they had a candidate who would accept the call, but twice they were disappointed. The leadership base was shrinking. The enthusiasm of the previous era began to give way to an emphasis on survival goals. A young Indian couple summarized the situation by greeting the new pastor with the words, "Six months later, and we would have handed you three empty buildings."

In April 1990 I came from twenty-one exciting and challenging years as pastor of a growing interracial congregation in the Midwest to this far more complex community setting for ministry. My wife and I were attracted by the challenge of work with a congregation that is composed of persons from many nations in a community that continues to serve as a port of entry for thousands of immigrants from all over the world. We saw this as a God-given opportunity to serve with people from a number of countries in Africa—Uganda, Togo, Ghana, Nigeria, Liberia, and Zaire— and those from Jamaica, Belize, Haiti, Trinidad, Antigua, and many other places as well as those of African-American and Anglo heritage. In particular, those of East Indian origin from Guyana had become a sizable part of the community.

But where to begin? A young African-American woman, a daughter of the first family of color to join in the 1950s, explained to the new pastor, "Your predecessor's role was to get people back into the buildings; yours is to help us shape a more effective instrument of mission."

Initially, I worked with the leaders to identify needs and establish priorities. The first was to restore worship to the exciting level it had been when my predecessor left and build on that. Because worship is always the focal point of the gathered people's life, preparation for worship became our number-one priority. The following steps were taken to ensure that worship became the experience of the congregation as a community of believers.

"Time with Our Children," led by members, was begun for the first time during the worship service. At least fifteen youth and adults have become highly visible to the congregation through providing leadership for this time. This time also reminds the congregation of our growing ministry with children as two to three dozen come forward.

The Worship and Music Committee also recognized the need for music to speak to the traditions of the multinational congregation. This is always a challenge, especially in a congregation whose tradition for over three centuries had been classical sacred music. The congregation sings vociferously, coming from rich music traditions. One well-received addition has been for a guitarist to lead the youngsters in a song at the end of the children's time, often with the congregation joining in the singing. The chancel choir remains at ten to fifteen, much too small for a congregation now averaging between 300 and 400 at worship. The choir director has invited members to join the choir for a short time for particular experiences such as Easter, and that has encouraged several more people to participate. Recently a young African American, a new member, and a middle-aged Guyanese began to assemble a contemporary choir using keyboard and guitar. Increasing the vitality of music in worship and involving more people in the music programs is identified as a high priority.

There is a time in worship that we call Concerns for God's Church and World. A layperson had usually read excerpts from the bulletin. Now the pastor has assumed this role and uses it as a time to highlight events in the congregation's life, to focus on people by name, to introduce visitors, to have individuals announce events, and to welcome back any who have been ill or traveling.

We have affirmed and continued the role of a lay liturgist and have expanded the roster of ushers to thirty plus a group of volunteer greeters. Youth of various ethnic backgrounds receive the morning offering as part of a larger strategy to give greater visibility to our multi-ethnic identity.

The second priority was to expand what had become a shrinking Sunday school. Recognizing that pastors teach by modeling, I accepted the leadership of the one adult class. It has grown from five to two dozen regular attenders. By the end of my second year, the total church school attendance had climbed to over a hundred.

Our third priority was to restructure the leadership base. That lean structure of the session plus two task forces was appropriate for the small congregation of 1974, but we had outgrown it. Those few leaders were becoming exhausted. Their overload was accentuated during that two-year period when there was no permanent pastor. That lean structure also offered few points of entry for the next generation of leaders. The elected board was at least two-thirds female, even though the congregation in the last decade had increased the male membership from 30 to 40 percent. Only three persons on the two boards (30 total members) were of Indian descent, even though one-third of our members came from that background. The leadership process had not provided a point of entry for new male members or those of non-African origin.

This leadership dearth anxiety had surfaced quickly in the Pastor Search Committee interview process. I suggested more session committees with opportunities for congregants at large to serve on them. By the time I arrived to begin my work, the session had in place seven committees instead of two: Christian Education, Congregational Life, Property Management, Evangelism and Church Growth, Stewardship/Finance, Worship/Music, and Mission Interpretation and Service. No session member is allowed to serve on more than one committee.

The next step was to expand our seven-day-a-week programming as a growing church with a community focus. We now offer more than two dozen programs, events, services, classes, and ministries every week. These include a soup kitchen feeding 175, vacation church school, male and female basketball teams, Girl Scouts, a women's support group, mid-week Bible study, a youth group, defensive karate classes, tactical narcotics team meetings, computer training, tutoring, narcotics anonymous, Alcoholics Anonymous, Al-Anon, a clothes closet, and Presbyterian men's and women's organizations.

This heavy use of what are now old buildings has created the need for another round of repairs and modernizing of our physical facilities. Fortunately, that and other needs can be financed at least in part by the income from wise investments made by the previous generations of leaders. Their foresight, combined with the wisdom of the contemporary leaders and the skills of our business administrator, has been a big factor in our continued ministry in this rapidly changing community.

The members were challenged nearly twenty years ago with the arrival of my predecessor. After two years of indecision during that vacancy period, they were ready to be challenged again. The burst of energy that came forth amazed both the members and me.

One of our highlights was our first Easter Sunday here. Nearly 800 people came. The experience of that crowded, enthusiastic worship experience convinced both the members and me that we were celebrating two resurrections that day. For some people one of the key statistics is in baptisms. The typical 600-member Presbyterian congregation reported approximately a dozen baptisms in 1991. We baptized 22 infants and 20 adults, ending the year with 635 members.

What Have We Learned?

Out of our experiences in multi-cultural congregations we have learned these lessons.

1. Multi-cultural congregations grow best by word of mouth as enthusiastic members share their story and their pilgrimage in God's community.
2. Multi-cultural congregations grow when leadership is shared and is representative.
3. Multi-cultural congregations grow when the community of faith is nurtured through worship, education, and fellowship in content and relationships.
4. Multi-cultural congregations grow as they serve.
5. Multi-cultural congregations grow when they extend a warm and genuine welcome to visitors from another culture.

We have also learned that a single-culture congregation moves to a multi-cultural identity through a combination of hope, vision, planning, prayer—and surprises. Among the central principles we have identified and can affirm are these:

1. The inclusive congregation has its identity grounded in biblical doctrine, especially that of reconciliation.
2. A healthy pride in diversity is nurtured.
3. Leadership is carefully planned, both clergy and lay.
4. Sociological factors are honestly studied and realistically understood, and these include:
   (a) availability of diverse people
   (b) peer identity for all
   (c) attractive, adequate facilities
   (d) accessible location in a nonthreatening setting
   (e) parking and security
   (f) membership of sufficient size to support quality worship, Christian education, pastoral care, service/advocacy
5. Structuring and planning in terms of growth patterns, visible leadership, and a variety of styles of worship are essential.

9.

Renewal Is Central

Kevin E. Martin

The bright Denver sunshine (three hundred days a year) radiates off the icy streets and snowy lawns. The quiet side streets around Christ Episcopal Church, Denver, begin to fill with the early morning crowd. People arrive early for the services at Christ Church. This way they can greet friends and still find a seat. As the time for the main service approaches, energy and a sense of anticipation grow in the congregation. Sunday morning at Christ Church is a highly meaningful event. Christ Church is not a typical Episcopal congregation. It has many younger families and early career singles. For a central-city congregation, there are many children. While many Episcopal congregations have been in decline in the Denver area, Christ Church has kept pace with the growth in the area's population. Many of these new members are drawn by the worship and preaching style. Christ Church is identified as a charismatic or Spirit-filled congregation. This is most exemplified by the presence of contemporary music and preaching with a strong emphasis on practical application of biblical principles. Other aspects of this emphasis are the strong commitment to prayer and particularly to the healing ministry.

Another key element of the strength of the congregation is its leadership. Christ Church has had only three rectors during its existence. The present rector and vestry are strongly committed to building ministry for the future. This parish illustrates the crucial importance of strong, future-oriented, persuasive, and challenging pastoral leadership. For many central-city churches today, that is the key variable between growth and decline.

Christ Church is only two miles from the geographical center of the city of Denver. It is in the university district, a few blocks from Denver University. The housing around Christ Church reflects the modestly successful older neighborhoods formed in the 1950s in Denver's rapid expansion after World War II.

How It All Began

It was during the mid 1950s that St. John's Cathedral, Denver, launched three new congregations in the rapidly expanding areas of the city. Christ Church was one of these. Today it rivals the parent congregation in both size and influence. The method of expansion used by the Cathedral was similar for all three newly formed congregations. A clergy staff member of the Cathedral organized families in the main congregation who lived in these expanding areas.

The Reverend Garret Barnes fulfilled this role for Christ Church, serving as the vicar of the newly formed mission and then as rector of the self-supporting congregation. His twenty-two-year tenure ran from 1952 to 1974. His strong, stable, and consistent leadership encouraged a time of growth and development. From its inception Christ Church had a high sense of commitment and volunteerism among its membership. The first rector gave these pioneers and builders permission to lead the church to growth and ministry.

By 1960 the congregation had grown to nearly 900 members. From the congregation's first gathering in a local school, the leadership carried out a series of successful building programs. In 1960 an extension was added to the modest church and parish hall built in 1954. This yielded a long, narrow, somewhat dark church that housed the congregation worship until 1990. The congregation added a Christian education complex in 1978.

The main church building allowed further growth, but its long narrow style and dark architecture also left members with a desire to upgrade the facilities. This dream was not fulfilled until 1990, the fifth year of the present rector, the Reverend Bruce McNab.

"It was very apparent to me that an immediate agenda for my rectorship was some improvement of the outgrown building." Bruce shared these comments as he reclined in his desk chair and reflected on his first years. "There was very little resistance to a new building. In fact, people were past ready to do something about it."

Bruce is the third rector of Christ Church. He followed the ten-year tenure of the Reverend David Wilson. "David built on the high sense of volunteerism. He introduced 'Renewal' and particularly a high commitment to lay ministry. This aspect of Renewal more than any other caught on here." Renewal is a general term that is used to describe a combination of elements found in the Charismatic movement in mainline congregations. The cornerstone of this movement is usually an emphasis on the supernatural empowerment of the Holy Spirit and the presence of various gifts, such as prophecy and tongues.

"I'm very grateful for the ground work he did. He was a former naval officer, a gifted counselor, and a good organizer." These are some terms that Bruce uses to describe his predecessor. Many Episcopal churches experience a radical change in the style of leadership when there is a change in the senior pastor. Christ Church has benefited from a strong sense of continuity.

The congregation continued to grow under David Wilson's leadership. This growth reached around 1,100 communicants in 1990. This continued growth only added more strain to the facilities and caused inadequate parking.

With Bruce McNab's arrival the congregation undertook a bold new building project. The new contemporary building was built over the shell of the old structure. The new worship space transformed the atmosphere of the congregation. From cavernous, dark, and long, the new building was bright, expansive, and lively. This new facility fits better the growing openness in Renewal worship, with an emphasis on contemporary music. The congregation sits in a semi-circular fashion, with both a choir and a music group located to the side to provide optimum leadership.

The new facility allowed the congregation to expand immediately. Today Christ Church is still growing, with 2,200 baptized members and 1,300 communicants, and an average between 690 and 750 attending Sunday morning services. Plans are being made to expand the administrative and classroom buildings to meet the continued growth. "Parking is our main problem," sighs Bruce. "We've got to do something about it!"

Why Do They Come?

What brings people to Christ Church? Who are the people who are attracted to this parish, which has sustained consistent growth for the past four decades?

"In a large church there is such variety! Kids can choose from many friends to find a group; youth activities include outstanding small discipleship groups, a music group, outreach trips and projects, and lots of fabulous role models." These are the words of a young mother of three school-aged children. "We are strongly in favor of the parish's practice of offering ministry to seventh and eighth graders," then with serious emphasis she adds, "a time when they are also making many other critical life decisions."

How important is Christ Church's emphasis on quality youth ministry to the parish's ongoing growth? "I just can't believe it. I now have thirty-one kids in my first-grade class. They come and they stay. They like what we offer." These words come from one of the two first-grade teachers.

Four emphases in programming mark Christ Church today. Each contributes to the synergism and energy that draw people from all over Denver to be part of this community. "First there is the worship and the preaching." The rector says with conviction in his voice, "I believe you must do the basics well." Worship at Christ Church reflects the rector's convictions. While using the 1979 prayer book of the Episcopal Church, the worship at Christ Church is very upbeat, lively, and spiced with a blend of traditional and contemporary music done with excellence. Contrary to the quieter, more traditional aspects of worship one usually finds in an Episcopal church, worship at Christ Church finds people clapping with the music, raising hands, and expressing a contagious joy.

Christ Church is identified as a "Renewal" or "Charismatic" congregation by other Episcopalians. "We haven't put much emphasis on the more spectacular verbal gifts," Bruce shares. "Our renewal is reflected more in our music and preaching."

Preaching and teaching are the primary skills that Bruce McNab sees in himself as the third rector. He puts a heavy emphasis on adult education and in his pulpit ministry. His style of preaching is strongly didactic, but spiced with energy and illustrations. Bruce's strong voice and imposing physical posture are a strong complement to the contemporary architecture.

A second strong programmatic thrust is education on all levels. The church school teaching core is a mixture of older, more mature lay leaders and newer people. This continues to draw younger families who, consistent with the profile of baby boomers, are concerned with quality education for themselves and their children.

A third emphasis is ministry in reaching the twenty- and thirty-year-old singles. Christ Church has a strong reputation for this ministry. A young ordained staff member, who obviously relates well to this constituency, leads this work. The congregation sees itself as providing a strong Christian ministry to this group to act as a counterculture to the secular cultural influences that pressure them. The presence of this program also may represent the growing transition of the neighborhood immediately surrounding the church. What about a ministry to the university? "We haven't been strong in this area," Bruce responds. "Our singles are more career and young professionals. We only get a few students. We should be doing more in this area."

A fourth program area is lay ministry. From its beginning through today, the congregation has stressed volunteerism both inside and outside the parish. Opportunities for involvement abound at Christ Church, from prayer groups and organizational ministries through a strong commitment to outreach. A reflection of this is Christ Church's support in money and people of the St. Francis Center, an ecumenical outreach mission to Denver's homeless and needy. "Our people are deeply involved with the Center," the rector shared. "It's much more than casual involvement. I hope to see us expand this in the year ahead, perhaps. We could challenge the congregation to give one dollar outside the congregation for each dollar we spend on ourselves."

Last, though not a formal program of the congregation, Christ Church has provided quality leadership to the wider church community. Members are very active in the leadership of the Episcopal Diocese of Colorado. This involvement ranges from elected diocesan leaders to an active youth leadership.

What about the future? Growing pains abound for this worshiping community. Facilities and parking need improvement. Plans are being made to expand outreach. "I think we could easily create a new mission, just as the Cathedral did in 1952," the rector stated. "Perhaps in fast-growing southern suburbs of Denver where we presently have no congregations." One senses that indeed they could.

Seven Lessons from Experience

What can we learn from this multi-faceted, spirit-filled congregation? Seven characteristics stand out most clearly.

1. The importance of strong pastoral leadership is crucial. This has been and remains strong at Christ Church. The present leadership of this congregation is clearly future-oriented. A high commitment to vision and planning is evident in all areas of the congregation's life.

2. A strong commitment to excellence also is central. One senses that Christ Church aims at first-class for everything. From music to outreach there is an expectation of excellence. New people want to be a part of this kind of community.

3. A strong adult education program is essential. This undergirds the commitment to high standards for membership. This is in strong contrast to the widespread low-commitment style of many Episcopal congregations.

4. The people of Christ Church believe the Holy Spirit is present and at work. They witness to this reality regularly. They want others to experience this spiritual reality.

5. This parish places an ongoing emphasis on growth, both in quantity and in quality of membership. This is a strong part of Christ Church's forward-looking leadership. Christ Church respects the past, but does not worship it.

6. People are challenged to serve. Members of Christ Church are constantly provided opportunity to do ministry. There is a spirit of anticipation that we can start new ministries to meet new needs.

7. The needs of the world around them are always kept before the people. Christ Church responds to the community. Whether this be the homeless or the needy or the single and the lonely, this community has a strong outward focus.

In summary, unlike so many central-city congregations, Christ Church has an optimistic future. It has become a magnetic congregation that looks to the future with excitement and anticipation. It has visionary leadership and a committed membership. Renewal has prepared this parish for the twenty-first century.

10.

God's Dream Was Bigger Than My Dream!

Norman Neaves

Back in 1968 when I moved to Oklahoma City to launch Church of the Servant, I had a dream in mind for the kind of church I would like it to be—and I thought if we could ever have a church that one day would have 400 members and a budget of $20,000, we really would have done something, and my ultimate dream would have been fulfilled.

Yes, that was 1968, and $20,000 then was the equivalent of $85,000 in 1992, but still you get the point. A congregation of that scope and that size would be worthy of my life's investment. I was prepared to do whatever I needed to do in order to make it happen. But guess what—on the very first Sunday we worshiped together, 200 people showed up, and 148 actually joined. Our offering on that first Sunday was $402, which, if multiplied by fifty-two Sundays, was already more than $20,000. And so, when I went home after our services that first Sunday, I was bewildered and deeply perplexed on the inside. Oh yes, I was excited and pumped up, for it was a wonderful thing—no doubt about it. But I was also bewildered and perplexed. And why? *Because my ultimate dream had been broken to pieces on that very first Sunday!*

I had spent the entire summer of 1968 going from house to house knocking on doors, beginning about 9:30 in the morning and finishing about 4:00 in the afternoon, and then going back in the evenings to meet with couples after the spouse got home from work. (It's amazing how few two-paycheck families there were in the late 1960s as compared to today!) In fact, I knocked on over 1,700 doors that summer in hopes of finding people who might be interested in beginning a brand-new and exciting congregation in the fall.

But it soon became apparent to me that I had better be careful in the kind of people I would be attracting to the new church. It was apparent that the major problem I faced was not one of getting people to respond, but rather in making sure that the majority of those people with whom we would begin the new venture were healthy personalities and not folks who were uninvolved in other congregations because of personal problems of their own. It wasn't long before I could see that a good many people interested in forming a new church often carry hidden agendas and personal problems that arose in previous church associations that would only make it difficult for us to form a solid foundation and get off to a promising start.

In other words, I began to realize it is probably wise to do selective recruitment rather than open evangelism in the first years of a new congregation's life, so that, after laying a solid foundation, the congregation itself can do real and very promising evangelism in the years to come.

Peter or Paul?

We also faced another challenge. We recognized that many people who were not meaningfully involved in another church were people who, for lack of a better way to describe it, were "secularists" of one sort or another. That is, the churches they had experienced at that time had not spoken relevantly to the newly emerging secular assumptions of the late 1960s. So, in addition to finding people who were emotionally healthy and also not involved in another congregation nearby, we felt "called" to develop a unique ministry that would reach out to more secularized young adults in urban America at that time. Our ministry, therefore, would be more in the tradition of the apologists in the history of the church rather than in the tradition of the dogmatists. It would be a ministry more like that of Paul, who reached out to the Gentiles of the world, rather than a ministry like that of Peter, who saw the faith as but a facet within the existing believing community.

Audience or Community?

Therefore, by the late fall of 1968 I stopped visiting and looking for new members. And I did it because I now had another fear mounting on the inside—not a fear of failing because I might not find anyone with whom to begin the new church, but now a fear of failing in developing a faithful and authentic community of believers rather than just a mass of spectators who were joining what could wind up being nothing more than just a religious club. That was when I became concerned, not so much with membership as with discipleship. I decided I must build a congregation, not simply an audience.

Since that time, we have not had an evangelism program at Church of the Servant. We have not called on visitors, gone knocking on doors, specifically asked people to join our church, or anything of the sort. What we have done instead is to find every way conceivable to freely and happily share the love of Christ with the community in which we find ourselves. We seek to discover hurts and ways to heal them. We try to find specific and concrete needs and identify ways to fulfill them. That is what we seek to do to the best of our ability, and with God's help our church has grown steadily and sometimes even dramatically, despite the absence of a traditional evangelism program.

When we were four months old, our membership numbered 302 people, and we had an average attendance on Sunday morning of 223. By 1973 our membership was over 900, and our average Sunday morning attendance passed 500. By 1983, our membership had grown to 2,100, and our attendance had gone over 1,100. We surpassed the 1,500 mark in Sunday morning attendance in 1987, and our membership that year reached 2,800. After twenty-three years of life together in Christ, our church's membership is now over 4,200 people with an average attendance in our services on Sunday morning of over 2,000 people and actual budget receipts of $2.4 million in fiscal 1991. Like it or not, we have become a regional church! People come to our community of faith from all over central Oklahoma, even driving on Sunday mornings from towns that are fifty to seventy-five miles away—not because we have had an evangelism program in place, not because we have tried to "get" more new members, but simply because we have tried to meet real human needs and touch real human hurts with the simple and compassionate ministry of Christ our Lord.

Membership or Discipleship?

Let me offer an example of what I am talking about. In 1978, the Reverend Bob Gardenhire came to our church to be our Minister of Pastoral Care. But it wasn't long until the two of us began to envision something different for his role—not the more usual role of one who visits the hospitalized and shut-ins and counsels those with personal burdens, but rather as one who facilitates the ministry of the laity in these areas—and what has happened in that area of ministry alone has been nothing short of a miracle. Bob put together his first "Care Team" within a year of becoming a part of our church staff. This was a team of eight laypersons whom he trained to form significant relationships with those in the hospitals. In time, these persons began extending the ministry of our church to those facing surgery or otherwise convalescing in the medical centers of our city. The bonding that took place between those doing the caring and those being cared for was remarkable—and it even began to be apparent in the larger life of our congregation itself! Additional care teams have been formed to carry on these ministries with the rapidly growing congregation. Today, between thirty and forty people in our church family handle this aspect of our church's ministry for us.

But other special groups were formed by Bob Gardenhire as well. He began training persons with appropriate gifts to be lay counselors in our church family, using his skill and expertise as a clinically trained pastoral supervisor to develop this phase of ministry in another group of our laity. Several of these laypersons have had college and graduate work in counseling psychology; others have not. But today those seventeen lay counselors will relate to more than 166 people in a given year, helping them work through personal crises of one sort or the other and make for themselves a new beginning in Christ. This ministry extends beyond the borders of our church membership, offering help and counsel and care to hundreds and hundreds of folks who are hurting whether they actually belong to our church or not. Today the ministry includes note writers, cookie bakers, affirmers, spiritual guides, and many other groupings of lay people who use their own unique and special gifts to be in ministry to others—more than 350 people in all, serving directly or indirectly close to 2,000 people in a given year!

More recently Bob and his lay associates opened an a new area of ministry—a healing ministry occurring one Sunday evening each month. Recently that ministry alone, which began with about fifty to sixty people in attendance, had more than 400 people in attendance for a service dealing with resentment in our lives and exploring ways for the healing touch of Christ to help us deal with that essentially spiritual problem. That particular evening, more than one-third of those present were not members of our church.

Today we have hundreds and hundreds of laypersons in our church family who are offering their gifts of love through our educational ministries, music ministry, youth and children's ministries, singles ministries, discipleship ministries, financial ministries, special kinds of adult ministries, and mission and outreach ministries. The spirit of being a servant church has caught on in the life of our congregation, the spirit of simply sharing the love of God and the compassion of Christ wherever and whenever and to whomever we can. In my opinion, it is evangelism—but not in traditional terms.

We have about forty people on our church staff, but we now realize that we cannot really do justice to the quality of our congregational life and the quality of our membership growth if we take in more than ten times that number of people in a given year. In other words, I have discovered that if we receive more than 400 people in our membership with a staff of our size, we will have substantial difficulty integrating and assimilating and nurturing those people into meaningful levels of discipleship. My preference is that the ratio between staff and new members in a given year be one to seven or one to eight, instead of one to ten. Usually we can work within that basic and healthy parameter if we let our growth be natural and not growth that we try to stimulate. By some standards our growth may not appear to be impressive when compared to other regional churches, but it is about all we can handle given our focus on discipleship rather than on membership.

To put that another way, if we had focused on membership growth and development over the past twenty-three years, doing everything we possibly could to hustle new members into the church, we probably would not have the kind of positive feeling about our future that we have today.

Growing with a Growing City

Oklahoma City is the fourth largest metropolitan area in the United States in square miles, covering twice the land area of New York City and nearly three times that of Chicago. It is larger than Dallas and Fort Worth combined and twelve times the size of Boston in land area. More than one million people reside in this metropolitan area, spread out over more than 600 square miles. You can find Church of the Servant people in large numbers in every quadrant of the city. That fact alone has had a major influence on our church's decision making with regard to relocating our facilities. Where should we build? How can we locate ourselves in such a way as to continue a strategic ministry to the thousands of people who now call us their church home?

Several years ago we studied carefully the demographics of our city and our membership concentration. We reluctantly realized that our six-acre tract of land simply was not enough to accommodate our growth. We must relocate. Since our people come from all over the metropolitan area, we first considered moving more toward the center of the geographic area of Oklahoma City. But it wasn't long until we discovered that was not feasible. For one thing, we found that a twenty- to twenty-five acre piece of land was not available other than in industrial districts. The cost of the few sites that were available turned out to be completely unaffordable. Where could we relocate in order to serve our people and the future growth of our church?

It finally dawned on us that the real issue we had to face was not geography so much as accessibility. We realized that we didn't need to locate more toward the center of the city, but rather at a place to which our people could drive easily and as quickly as possible. So we began to look at the choice of our new site with a new pair of eyes.

After doing significant studies involving the state Department of Transportation and the Oklahoma City Planning Commission and other such groups, we found the ideal location for our church and its ministry for the twenty-first century.

After considering fourteen different pieces of property, we chose the one best suited for the kind of congregation we believe God is leading us to become. It is located in northwest Oklahoma City in an area that today is virtually unpopulated. The critical variable is not the distance from the center of the city, but the fact that the north outer loop in Oklahoma City, a major thoroughfare connecting all other expressways and bypasses and turnpikes in central Oklahoma, is now being constructed. It passes within 400 yards of our new location! Not only will we be accessible to people living in every area of metropolitan Oklahoma City, but also most of those people coming from great distances will be able to get to our newer location faster and easier than to our present one. We believe we have chosen a piece of property that not only functionally meets the criterion of the church we are and the church we are becoming, but also will continue to convey the metropolitan and regional "feel" we believe it should have. It is the perfect location for us at this juncture in our development. Truly we are poised to meet the challenge of our future!

We are constructing a 100,000-square-foot facility as our first unit, but undoubtedly we'll be ready to consider our next unit in two or three years after completion of the first one. We also have initiated a joint venture with the YMCA in Oklahoma City whereby we are giving them a piece of our property upon which to construct a major branch for far northwest Oklahoma City. The YMCA will construct the building at their expense, and yet we will be able to use the facility on Sunday mornings for adult and youth educational spaces. Their building and our building have been designed by the same architect and have the very same appearance. We feel that the church will bring many new members to the Y and that the Y in turn will help to enhance the church's visibility and indirectly facilitate the church's growth. We will be in partnership with each other and expect to stimulate our respective ministries. Thus our partnership will involve not only a joint venture in sharing common property, but also a joint venture in ministering to the whole person.

Finally, I must acknowledge that the greatest breakthrough of my entire ministry and life in the faith came when I realized that ministry is not something we create nor something we make happen. Ministry is something that is God's doing and that the Lord entrusts to us in the hopes that we will be faithful to it. The secret to a fulfilling ministry, it has finally dawned on me, lies not in the images and plans and strategies that I concoct nor in the mere human designs that come out of my own mind and my own limited understandings. The secret to a fulfilling ministry lies in being able to get out of the way and let God's dream begin to emerge—and then to discern that dream clearly enough and to serve that dream faithfully enough that it does justice to what God has in mind.

This is not intended to be a pietistic statement. It is a deep and burning spiritual conviction that has come to me over the last two decades while trying to be in ministry in a given place. And so the question for us has not to do with whether we will be a regional church. The critical question is whether we will take the necessary steps and structure ourselves in such a way that we can continue to let God work in us and through us to accomplish the plans and the dreams that God has in mind. In other words, Church of the Servant does not belong to me and it does not belong to all of us who make up its membership either. It belongs to God and to God alone. It is an instrument in the Lord's hand. And it is not for us to choose the kind of future we want; we must be faithful to the future that God has chosen.

A regional church? Yes, I guess that's what we are, but that has never been my goal. A faithful church and a relevant church and a church that loves the world on behalf of its Lord? I can only hope that, in some small way, that's what we are and what we will continue being in the years to come.

11.

From Chapel to Regional Church

Roger O. Douglas

One of our members, a strict fundamentalist from the South, commented, "St. Philip's has some of the most conservative, as well as some of the most liberal church people I have ever encountered. St. Philip's seems to thrive on and encourage a wide theological spectrum. There are groups where charismatics feel comfortable and others where social-action types flourish. The rector keeps saying that we need not all be of one mind, as long as we are of one heart."

A former Methodist, who moved to Tucson from Michigan, said, "I was drawn to St. Philip's because of its sense of holiness and tradition. The pomp and circumstance were there, but, at the same time, this was obviously a church for the twenty-first century."

A journalist who had not attended church since childhood commented, "I was always religious, but I kept putting off church membership. Most churches seemed to only pay lip service to social outreach. Then one day I interviewed the leader of the homeless in our city. I asked him what local church had been the most involved. He immediately said, 'St. Philip's. They would be willing to go to jail with us.' I knew that St. Philip's was where I belonged."

These comments stem from a multitude of changes and a diversity of concepts that St. Philip's has introduced or experienced in preparation for the twenty-first century.

With a membership of 1,400 families, a staff of twelve (four clergy), and five Sunday worship services attended by 1,200 people, St. Philip's is known as an Episcopal parish that has preserved the past while adapting and changing with the times.

Among the changes is a multi-faceted music program that includes seven adult or youth groups that involve more than 100 parishioners at four of the five Sunday services.

Our ecumenical involvement has grown from nearly nil to a role of leadership. Our first effort was with other Episcopal churches in the organization of a soup kitchen, giving parishioners an opportunity to make contact with the city's transients and the chronically mentally ill, as well as abused women. It was a prelude to our present leadership role in the Pima County Interfaith Council, which was conceived in the late 1980s by the Roman Catholic Diocese of Tucson. This broad-based organization, which includes Protestant, Catholic, and Jewish communities, addresses the urban issues of Tucson and Pima County.

As our outreach continued, we began taking on an educational project with Yaqui Indian children, a literacy program, work with refugees from Central America, and providing a place for homeless men to sleep on cold nights. The parish also adopted a sister church in San Salvador.

We quickly determined to make use of all available church space seven days a week and invited diverse community groups—including Twelve-Step groups, cultural organizations, Hispanic societies, nursing groups, and community college classes—to make St. Philip's their home base.

Then, within the parish we started many need-driven programs. Examples of these were a nursery school, a senior citizens' day, a counseling center—in all, forty-two internal groups are in operation—everything from crafts to a workshop concerning divorce, to a grief group and single-parent support group.

How Did We Get Here?

This congregation was started in 1936 by a unique visionary. The Reverend George Ferguson came to Tucson to winter, with no intention of planting a church. After several months of worshiping at the one Episcopal church in town, he was approached by some of the members to begin a new parish.

"No," he replied, "I'm not interested in a regular parish, but I would be happy to settle down in Tucson and have a chapel in my home. It would be good to worship in an intimate setting with my friends."

A local developer who was trying to sell land in the sparsely settled foothills offered Ferguson ten acres, the use of his architect, and a construction crew at cost if he would reconsider and build a chapel in the foothills. A small architectural gem was built, seating about 100 people, and Ferguson proceeded to hold services for his friends. At first, there was no typical Episcopal structure. Even many years later, the vestry (governing board) was known as "George's camera club." (Instead of regular monthly meetings, it was said that they went out to the desert, took pictures, and sometimes ended with a party at the Ferguson house.) In spite of the rector's original intentions, the congregation grew. People began to come from all over town, so Ferguson conceived of a plan to start satellite chapels in several areas of the city, allowing friends to gather at locations readily accessible to their homes. Through the years, three of these satellite chapels became thriving parishes on their own.

Eventually, Ferguson was replaced by Joseph Heistand, whose primary task was to bring this parish into the Episcopal orbit. Under Heistand, many commissions and committees were established, and a close diocesan relationship was forged. Parishioners of St. Philip's served in key positions within the diocese, and the parish began to support national church projects. Heistand helped the parish become a more recognizable medium-sized Episcopal institution, and after eight years as rector, he was elected Bishop of the Diocese of Arizona.

By 1977, when I was elected the third rector, this small Arizona town had become a thriving Southwestern metropolis. Tucson's population expanded from 30,000 in the 1930s to more than 400,000 in the 1980s, and the edge-of-town corner on which the small chapel had been built had become a landmark in the geographical center of one of the fastest-growing areas in America.

My initial problem as rector was how to bring this very comfortable Episcopal congregation, which was known to include many of the well-to-do and prided itself on its many art objects and a reputation for architectural beauty, into a more dynamic posture that was open to the Christian challenges of an expanding city. We decided to help people dream and then help them act out their dreams.

Learning to Dream

We began in parish neighborhood meetings, asking, "What is God asking this particular group of Christians to do in Tucson?"

As the parish again began to grow significantly, the concept of a metropolitan parish emerged from our combined dreams. We would cover the city and beyond. No longer would we be associated with one area or one class of people. The chapel model under the original rector had made for a more homogeneous and geographic grouping (which church growth experts have often recommended for expansion), but as land and resources became scarce, people no longer limited their associations to a neighborhood. The more St. Philip's thought of itself as a metropolitan parish, the more it embraced diversity.

Reenvisioning the Parish

As our vision expanded and new people and programs appeared, we began to speak of ourselves as "the cathedral" of Tucson—a church for the whole city. No longer were we concentrating on reaching out only to Episcopalians.

Sunday morning worship needed to be redesigned with an emphasis on variety and accessibility. The concept of making our services "user-friendly" was introduced. This necessitated reworking our bulletin, producing easy-to-use service booklets. (In most Episcopal parishes, one has to balance a prayer book, a hymnal, and a bulletin. Three-handed people are easily assimilated!) We also changed much of the language that is usually associated with Episcopal worship services. Our liturgy in the Episcopal Church is our greatest blessing as well as our greatest curse. Old-line Episcopalians have great problems whenever one tinkers with the liturgy. At the same time we were making changes in the service, we were also expanding the facilities and installing a new organ.

An outgrowth of this cathedral concept was increased efforts in a ministry to the community. The Reverend Paul Buckwalter, whose background was in community organization, was employed to spend half of his time working with secular agencies and the other half training our people for ministry in the city.

Buckwalter soon introduced parishioners to the "plunge" experience. These were two-day intensive explorations into the heart of the city to involve members of the congregation with street people, the courts, and social agencies. As people became more sensitive to the problems of the city, they began to say things like what was heard from one woman, "I've been living in Tucson for thirteen years, and I feel as if I've never been out of my neighborhood. St. Philip's has made me aware on a person-to-person level of my responsibility for the poor of the city."

The Price We Paid and Our Response

All of this signified a new direction and focus and resulted in a number of old-timers leaving to go to more traditional Episcopal churches. However, the gains in enthusiasm and hospitality far exceeded the losses, and we continued to attract some new people.

At this stage, we added another new staff member whose sole task was to nurture and facilitate the assimilation of newcomers to the parish. New members were encouraged to become a part of parish life, and five weekly classes for newcomers were cycled through the Sunday schedule. Special holidays were seen and planned as entry points (i.e., special times when nonchurch people or "church shoppers" would be present).

As we faced the problem of assimilating new members, we were forced once again to reimage our community.

In 1989, I was introduced to Carl George, Director of the Charles E. Fuller Institute for Evangelism and Church Growth. George accurately described our situation and suggested the "Meta-church" model as a response to large-church problems. Meta-church is a way of reconceptualizing the parish by seeing it primarily as small groups with times during which all the groups come together for worship and celebration. This model grows larger by intentionally focusing on smaller life-sharing groups that are, in effect, little churches within the greater church. The parish eagerly adopted this model, while maintaining many of the traditional groups and older systems. The clergy put much time and energy into training leaders and learning to manage ministry, rather than being the primary care-givers in the parish.

One of the principles that Carl George has introduced to us is the concept of the "empty chair." Each cell group maintains an open chair with the expectation that some newcomer or stranger will soon occupy the seat. This keeps cells from becoming ingrown and encourages them to multiply when they reach an unwieldy number of participants (usually about ten).

An important aspect of Meta-church thinking is the expanded role that Sunday mornings have taken. We now see Sundays as a celebration of cell groups and an opportunity for reconnecting the community. We have added extra services to meet the variety of needs of cell groups.

And we now intersperse the worship services with a variety of classes, meetings, rehearsals, and community forums.

Forums at 9:00 A.M usually are about family concerns, and those at 10:15 A.M. are about community issues, political concerns, and outreach projects. Classes are about moral and ethical problems, the nature of Anglicanism, Bible study, and training sessions for a variety of ministries. Some cell groups also meet on Sundays. With two Sunday schools every Sunday morning, an increasing number of people come for several hours to participate in what some call our "mall" model.

Resistance Intensifies

It was at this point that the strongest resistance was felt. The phenomenon of shifting the emphasis from internal to external, from focusing on ourselves to others outside the parish, began to be perceived in negative terms. Old-timers complained about all the new faces that were seen on Sundays and the lack of parking; many of the traditional fellowship groups felt threatened.

"We always used to have the clergy spend time at our meetings," complained one of the original members who started with Ferguson. "Now they are always downtown. I think we're getting too political. The clergy seem to have lost the pastoral touch. Why, they never seem to visit unless you've got a big problem." The parish also began to be viewed with suspicion and hostility by the diocese. As the cathedral image took hold, less support was given to the diocese. The general feeling in the parish was for greater decentralization of decisions and more importance on local outreach causes. More money flowed toward city projects and less toward denominational concerns.

The blurring of diocesan loyalties at St. Philip's underscores one of the characteristics of many growing center-city churches. Buckwalter, St. Philip's outreach clergy, explained this change: "We are an Episcopal church, but not deeply rooted in denominational work. Local parishioners and clergy have a better understanding than a committee in Phoenix of the needs of Tucson."

Through the years, the tension has grown between St. Philip's and the diocese. One parishioner expressed his concern, "The diocese is only interested in the survival of the bureaucracy and keeping small places going. All they seem to say is, 'Keep quiet and send us your money.' "

Many parishes like St. Philip's have moved away from the collision course toward a coalition course. They have joined networks of similar-sized parishes for mutual support and the furtherance of the mission of the Church. These new coalitions often cross both regional and denominational lines. They exist to meet the parish needs and overcome the sense of loneliness that often overtakes large-church clergy who are out of step with their denomination or diocese. For us, as for scores of very large congregations, local, regional, and national interchurch coalitions are replacing the old unilateral intra-denominational relationships.

The Changing Role of Governance

Another outgrowth of the size increase has been the gradual change in the governance of the church. Reducing the vestry's meeting times to only four a year, we reprogrammed the vestry function to focus on the big picture of the parish mission and long-range planning rather than day-to-day corporate affairs. Many of the administrative decisions formerly handled by the vestry are now in the domain of an executive committee, consisting of the rector, the executive pastor, an administrator, and the senior and junior wardens (laypeople). The executive committee distributes minutes of its meetings to the vestry and staff and provides information that sets the agenda for the vestry's quarterly meetings.

The quarterly vestry meetings are in a retreat format and last for two days. The emphasis in these retreats is on building community and spiritual growth. As we act our size, we, like other big congregations, encourage our busy members to focus on doing ministry, rather than assuming administrative duties.

Concluding Remarks

This chapter is the story of one center-city church that has evolved and redefined its role from a chapel to a regional parish. In other ways, however, it has stayed the same and simply grown in size and scope. The appeal has grown from strictly an Episcopal-based to a more general-church following; many lapsed mainline Protestants and Catholics have found St. Philip's to be their spiritual home.

Four principles that have come out of the last fifteen years seem to me to be the bedrock to a growing church in today's central cities:

1. The leadership of a city church must have a hunger for innovation combined with a healthy respect for the past. We must not rest on our laurels; yet we must be willing to honor the past and build on the contributions of the former clergy. As the familiar adage goes, "What goes around comes around."
2. In the 1950s the relationship to the denomination was stronger than the ties to the community. Today that set of loyalties must be reversed.
3. The leadership must be vision-driven. It must have the willingness to reshape an institution and challenge the conventional wisdom regarding churches that often comes from old paradigms.

4. The leadership must be in for the long haul. Too often clergy like to make changes and look for instant cures. Change within a large church takes time, and the more established the church, the longer one needs to prepare the congregation for new dreams to emerge.

Over the years, many changes have taken place at St. Philip's, yet there never has been a time when we have settled back and felt we have "arrived." We have a strong sense of our imperfections and a vision that the best days lie ahead of us in the coming century.

12.

The Best Mediocre Church Around

Randy Rowland

"We are one of the best mediocre churches around," said Bruce Larson in describing University Presbyterian Church of Seattle while he was pastor there.

Larson went on to say, "There are no excellent churches."

While some churches and church leaders might be offended by such a statement, most of the core members of this 3,550-member urban congregation would agree.

University Presbyterian Church has existed for eighty years in its present location. The church was founded when a visionary group of men and women who lived in the university district of Seattle purchased some property and got the blessing of Seattle's First Presbyterian Church to found a new congregation. Its mission was to serve the university and professional community. This has been and continues to be the church's passion. There is an internal humility in the congregation that recognizes it does not achieve its mission perfectly.

This is a church that is working hard to be relevant yet uncompromising with the good news of Jesus Christ. We don't always do either extremely well.

In an attempt to be open and welcoming toward people of diverse cultures and faith styles who are becoming Christians, rediscovering faith, or growing toward a profound faith, we are sometimes soft on aspects of the Christian faith other than primary doctrines. To offset this tendency, we have excellent adult fellowship groups, adult education classes, and small-group experiences that are discipleship and growth enhancers.

The congregation's new senior pastor, Earl Palmer, is a brilliant biblical expositor, and his presence will help us guard against theological compromises. Palmer recently declared, "My goal is to encourage ordinary Christians to become biblical Christians who understand the source of their faith and who seek to live out the gospel at home and work. The consequence of this is that we fulfill the deployment aspect of the gospel, helping people to discover their place of ministry in the world."

So, while this is not the most doctrinaire congregation in the country, we are sufficiently theologically centered to be a viable church for the theologically and biblically informed, yet always poised for ministry that is attractive to those who are socially conscious. A rhythm and balance is created between theological reflection and active ministry to the world.

While mediocre in avoiding compromise, we are also mediocre in being relevant. Although we have huge youth, college, and young adult ministries, we are focused around worship that caters largely to the previous generation with classical music and liturgy. Youth, college, youth adult, and contemporary worship meetings offer some options to the status quo, but we are clearly not a baby boomer-style ministry.

Earl Palmer, the new senior minister, has always desired to meet people where they are and make the gospel story come alive: "My conviction is that if I can get people to consider the texts of the Old and New Testaments, then Jesus Christ will authenticate himself. The Holy Spirit then makes Christ continually relevant."

Being a good mediocre church in the current religious and cultural climate is not easy. In fact, mediocrity is a hard standard to attain if you consider how hard it is to balance all the critical variables that determine church success or failure. Many Christian leaders are convinced that all of our successful mainline urban churches are a bad decision or two, a style element or two, a philosophical item or two away from becoming the empty monuments to that past glory that so many urban churches have become. It's not easy to achieve mediocrity. It seems almost unattainable to be excellent. But there are some elements that keep University Presbyterian Church alive, relatively healthy, and growing. These elements are an enthusiastic style, a relational focus, a strong focus on ministry, a kingdom focus, and community context awareness.

Enthusiastic Style

University Presbyterian Church is a congregation with a celebrative style of worship. Every worship service exudes energy. Music, large crowds, and the freedom to express joy make it a fun place to be on Sunday morning or evening. The enthusiasm comes from the pastoral staff and key leadership. One example is that the congregation often applauds a good musical performance or a moving personal story in our weekly "witness" interview, wherein members of the church share what is going on in their faith adventure with Christ. Meanwhile, another significant church in our area that is experiencing drastic decline has voted to ban clapping in church. Celebration allows for a little fun as people affirm the active presence of God in their lives.

One sage wisely said that every great success is born of some great enthusiasm. A church that attains mediocrity has to have energy and enthusiasm. Most of the staff would be at University Presbyterian Church on any given Sunday for worship, fellowship, and educational opportunities if it fell outside of their job description and went unpaid. The staff and elders, along with other key leaders, sincerely believe that God is there to meet us on Sundays in a way that is unique from how we experience God the rest of the week. The atmosphere is filled with expectation and excitement that permeates the building.

Relational Focus

People count. In our church there is a place for everyone. A person does not have to have it all together to be a part of the action and make a difference. One need not be theologically trained, arduously screened, or socially perfect to participate in ministry. This congregation is in the people building business. Helping people to see that they are "becomers"—men and women on a journey toward wholeness in Christ—is a central focus of the church.

A climate of acceptance, love, and cooperation is pervasive at this church. Our goal is to offer a safe place for people to tell their life story, discuss their faith journey, and take risks in ministry that are life changing. Small groups, short-term missions, fellowship groups, classes, and seminars have a relational focus that endeavors to bring out the very best in people. The leadership readily proclaims that Jesus Christ did not give his life on the cross for piety, theological or political precision, church buildings, or peppy programs. Jesus Christ died for people. People count at this church.

Ministry Focus

Lay ministry is what makes things happen at University Presbyterian church. Most of the pastors believe that most of the people in the groups they serve could do the pastors' jobs. The people of this church are truly competent ministers. Laypeople are giving of their time and resources in ways that are astounding. A divorced single mother is lead facilitator on a team that helps run our divorce recovery program. She and her team recruit small-group leaders, arrange curriculum and speakers, and host the meetings and a celebration dinner each quarter. This ministry serves over 300 people per year and is masterfully run by a layperson with no seminary training. In fact, her congregation of Christian and not-yet-Christian persons wounded by a terrible life event is larger than the average church in America. Just a few short years ago, this woman was experiencing the pain of her own divorce and knew nothing of ministry. This woman is one of the outstanding ministers of the church, and her competence is acknowledged.

While the church leadership believes in quality nurture, solid theological underpinnings, and the development of biblically informed social and moral responsibility, our key focus is ministry. The church slogan, which appears on the bulletin reads, "EVERY MEMBER A MINISTER." It is printed and repeated throughout the church. People do not learn theology to become intellectually or biblically sound merely for the sake of being sound. People learn theology and Bible in order to be equipped for ministry to the world.

One recent estimate is that nearly 2,000 of our members are directly involved in volunteer ministry. Many of those have chosen call-driven, intentional vocational paths such as teaching in our troubled public schools as their life's ministry.

Ministry is not just in-church. Ministry is to the world. We love ushers and greeters and parking attendants. Those jobs are important. But what the church really affirms is those lay ministers who are out there in the thick of the world—helping street kids, evangelizing through Young Life, running a halfway house for the mentally ill, staffing AIDS hospices, and feeding the hungry. These women and men are modern-day heroes of the faith. Like Mother Teresa, these everyday people are fulfilling the call of the gospel to be world changers and are making "something beautiful for God."

The Sunday bulletin logo reads: "sharing, shaping, caring, going." This is a place where sharing is central to the life of the covenant community. The first gift that is shared is members' various life and faith stories. Each is unique. Everyone has a story to tell, and the members become empowered as they tell stories and listen to the stories of others.

Shaping means that the church members are committed to becoming the men and women God has called them to be in Scripture.

Caring says that members make a serious attempt to take care of each other, recognizing that everyone has hurts and struggles. The church takes this caring very seriously. This is a celebrating community, but in the midst of the celebrating, people are encouraged to be very real. An important lesson has been learned: God uses people when they are up and when they are down, through success and in the midst of failure.

Going means that the life of faith ultimately involves risks. We must put our comfort and safety on the line and follow

Christ into the midst of a bleeding and broken world. We preach, proclaiming the necessity of risks.

Kingdom Focus

People do not come to University Presbyterian Church to fulfill a pastor's or program director's dream to make the church large and successful. Instead, people come with locked-up dreams for ministry. The job taken on by the staff is to help people clarify and then live out their dreams for ministry.

It does not matter where people go to do ministry as far as this church is concerned. In fact, in the last ten years this congregation has helped form or redevelop three neighboring churches by sending members out. We have many friends and members who actually help run programs in other churches. That's fine. We just want people to discover their gifts, articulate their unique dreams, and then go "do it."

Part of the process of enabling persons to do their dreams is offering opportunities to learn about the Christian faith. Sunday morning fellowship and education classes offer opportunities for both informational and experiential enrichment. In these courses persons are allowed to participate freely. Many grow in leadership skills and others discover teaching gifts that they are able to later utilize outside of University Presbyterian Church. The church also offers the community a midweek Bible study.

University Presbyterian is very open to offering its strong teaching, recovery, and fellowship ministries to the community for the greater good of the church at large in the Seattle area.

This is what is called a kingdom focus. The church never blatantly attempts to grow numerically by developing catchy programs or by retaining all the person power available inside the church.

Community Context Awareness

Any successful church has to ask at least two key questions: Whom do we serve? How do we serve them?

University Presbyterian Church is a metropolitan training center (one of the major church types, like suburban and rural). That means it draws its membership from a wide geographic area, there is significant turnover, there is a focus on empowerment, and the church tends to cater to persons who are: (1) burned out from other churches; (2) hurt by other churches; (3) exploring the Christian faith for the first time; (4) coming back to the church after a long hiatus; (5) hungry to learn about ministry, theology, and so on; and (6) are from the educational and professional community.

In answer to the second question of how to serve the constituents, University Presbyterian Church serves the people whom God sends by offering connections with others in similar life settings. The church serves them by creating a safe place in which to struggle, suffer, and overcome debilitating life problems while simultaneously gaining biblical and theological content and being encouraged to take risks in ministry. That means the church does not even try to keep all these people forever. In fact, we lose about 300 members per year (and expect that to continue) to other churches, death, and geographic relocation.

13.

A Citywide Church with a Worldwide Ministry

Robert G. Borgwardt

Berkeley, California, and Madison, Wisconsin, stood out during the turbulent 1960s as the university cities with highly visible student protests. The unrest on the campus in these two cities made national news. The most dramatic episode in the rebellion against traditional authority structures occurred in Madison when a science building was bombed and a graduate student was killed by the explosion. Other expressions of the student rebellion included peace marches, strikes, the so-called sexual revolution, drug abuse, and teach-ins.

From a larger context the religion editor of the *Wisconsin State Journal* wrote a provocative article on November 16, 1969, headlined: "Downtown Churches, Victims of a Trend." The writer pointed out that downtown churches throughout the country were in serious trouble. The changing demographics of the inner city, the flight of people to the suburbs, and the growth of strong suburban churches were cited as major factors in the assault on "Old First Church."

Perhaps the most complex political setting for the churches today is in those communities that are the home for both the state capital and the major state university. That short list includes Madison, Lincoln (Nebraska), Columbus (Ohio), and Austin (Texas).

The most common response of the downtown church during the second half of the twentieth century was to grow older and smaller. A second was to relocate to a more hospitable setting. A third, but far less common, response to the turmoil was to accept the role of a regional church and expand the variety of ministries.

Bethel Lutheran Church in Madison is both a downtown church and a university parish. For more than a century membership included business leaders, undergraduates, professors, politicians, graduate student families, university administrators, government employees, blue-collar workers, accountants, and a representative cross-section of the metropolitan population.

How was Bethel Lutheran Church able to grow and to become an innovative force in American Protestantism and around the world in such a tumultuous setting?

The Evolution of an Immigrant Parish

Part of the answer can be found in the roots. Before the Civil War, a small group of Norwegian immigrants gathered in rented rooms in Madison to break bread and share the cup. A Lutheran congregation with strong Norwegian roots was organized in 1855. Its first house of worship was built in 1863, four blocks from the Wisconsin State Capitol and in the shadow of the University of Wisconsin. By 1895, more than 200 members had adopted the name Bethel Lutheran Church.

From such humble beginnings one of the most dynamic immigrant-tested churches began its ministry. Originally the worship and educational efforts were held in the native Norwegian language of its members. However, with increasing pressure from an American society tempered by World War I, a full English program was provided by 1920.

A new chapter in Bethel's history began with the decision in 1922 to relocate. The new site on the isthmus between Lake Mendota and Lake Monona was just two blocks from the state capitol and a matching distance from the University of Wisconsin's Fraternity Row. However, because of economic stress and the Great Depression, construction proceeded in stages. It was not until 1941 that the beautiful English Gothic sanctuary seating 600 was completed.

When this sanctuary was ready for use, a veteran member told the pastor, "Bethel can do anything that it sets its mind to," then quickly added, "that is, only if that mind is in harmony with the purpose of God."

Under dynamic pastoral and lay leadership following World War II, Bethel continued to reach out to the American society. The church sanctuary was expanded in 1956. In 1963 the seating was increased to 1,300 and a large parish house for Sunday school, adult fellowship, and music and youth programs was completed. In that year, the last two houses were purchased on what had become the "Bethel Block" in downtown Madison. One house was removed and the other became a parish shop. The parish shop program was staffed by hundreds of volunteers.

Remodeling of the parish house and youth center was completed in 1986 to accommodate the changing nature of Bethel's congregation. The expansion was necessitated not only by expanding education needs, but also by the response of members and staff to societal ills and needs in downtown Madison.

In the midst of the stress-filled Vietnam War days, the baptized membership passed the 7,000 mark. In 1972 a demographic study determined that more than 60 percent of those members came from neither a Norwegian nor a Lutheran family heritage.

A pivotal expression of that veteran member's optimistic statement came in the mid-1950s when this parish adopted as its role "A Citywide Church with a Worldwide Ministry." That may sound like a modest statement today, but in the 1950s most churches defined their role in other ways. That immigrant parish had become a congregation with the world as its focus. A real test of the rhetoric came in the 1960s as absolutes were denounced as irrelevant options. Students, faculty, and large segments of the community revolted against the mindlessness and suffering of the Vietnam War. The sexual revolution began to erode the standards of decency and family life. But Bethel did not turn to a fundamentalist approach. Rather, it faced head-on in pulpit and educational thrust the challenges to the basic fundamental stance of the Christian faith. In a university town with more than 135 Ph.D.s in its membership and thousands of students worshiping in its sanctuary, Bethel faced the challenge of a growing secular society.

The Operational Expression of That Slogan

How has Bethel implemented that challenging vision? One response has been in the sermons that addressed both the public issues of the day and matters of personal faith.

A second is that for a quarter of a century Bethel men have

met Friday mornings from 7:00 to 8:00 for breakfast and exciting discussions on matters of religion and current events. They still meet, young and old, of various backgrounds—doctors, professors, students, government employees, businessmen. This hour has become precious to them. More than 200 men have been involved in this group, with forty to fifty as an average attendance. They were given free reign to focus on each other's life, faith, the assumptions by which they lived, and the challenges that face them in their personal lives and in their society.

Not only did the Sunday morning sermons focus and motivate, but adult forums, Bible studies, and weekly discussion groups all opened the minds of the congregation to the possibility of their Christian faith confronting the stresses and strains of modern life.

The most widely known expression of that slogan is the Bethel Bible Series. In the late 1950s this innovative approach to Bible study was created by an associate Bethel minister, Harley Swiggum. This pioneering, and widely copied, model has reached more than 100,000 teachers who in turn have taught students in exciting two-year classes. From 1965 to 1975, the program was shared with Christian people throughout our country as well as in Japan and Korea and at United States military bases in Australia and Europe.

Working in cooperation with the university campus pastors and other Lutheran congregations in the area, Bethel continued to challenge the students and faculty of the university community with lively worship and programs. In addition, the church counseling program was initiated in 1960 with full-time pastoral guidance as well as the professional support of psychiatrists and psychologists from the community.

A ministry to those with handicapping conditions was put in place in the 1970s, and two houses were purchased and maintained for year-round use by mentally handicapped men.

Bethel also became the home of a most exciting program for the elderly. Through the enthusiasm and skill of a Bethel staff member, the XYZ Center (Xtra Years of Zest) brought meaning and purpose to the lives of many older people. Seven hundred to a thousand people have participated in this program.

In addition, a large section of the remodeled Bethel complex was set aside in 1986 as an adult day-care center ministering to many older people in the community who otherwise would have been institutionalized or become a heavy family burden.

The Megachurch Role

One of the most significant trends in American Protestantism is that the very large urban churches gradually accept many of the responsibilities once carried by denominational agencies and more recently by parachurch organizations. The prime example at Bethel was the creation of the Bethel Bible Series.

A second came in the late 1960s when a 475-acre parcel of land near the Governor Dodge State Park was purchased. This camp, Bethel Horizons, services a huge constituency including youth from Bethel as well as from community, school, and other groups. One example is the summer program for nearly 230 young people from dysfunctional families in Dane County, Bethel's home county. In addition, a meaningful and well-conceived environmental studies program was set up under the full-time guidance of a staff naturalist. A recent addition to the camp was a ropes course, used by a number of congregations, businesses, and school districts to build self-esteem and a sense of interdependence among participants.

A third expression of the slogan that calls Bethel to serve a larger constituency is the human family project, a response to the disintegration of the family. This program places emphasis on human beliefs, human values, and human relationships. With the cooperation of key people from the University of Wisconsin and under the leadership of a university child psychiatrist and the Bethel pastors and members, the program has developed "The Born to Belong" course with seven videos, lectures, textbooks, teacher's manual, and trial discussions. Results so far have been encouraging. Bethel is now testing this program with other congregations in the Midwest. Bethel people are convinced that it addresses the fundamental crisis in the American home in an intelligent, rational, and scriptural manner.

One of the most highly visible expressions of this acceptance of a regional or megachurch role is illustrated by Bethel's long use of radio and television to spread the gospel. Bethel began to broadcast its Sunday morning worship services in 1942. Twenty years later, it began Saturday evening telecasts. They were shown in prime time, packaged with the news, weather, and sports program of a local television station. The telecasts were later aired by stations in three other Wisconsin cities.

In 1982, Bethel began broadcasting its Sunday morning services. The theme remained "the camera's view over the shoulder of the person in the pew." The broadcast's twofold purpose was to reach out to those who had no church home as well as to those who did but for various reasons of health or age were unable to worship there on a given Sunday morning.

Why Has It Worked?

Why has Bethel been able to grow to an average worship attendance of nearly 2,000 in such a challenging setting? Five factors stand out above all others.

First, this parish has been served by only five senior pastors since 1906, with the fifth being installed in the fall of 1991. These senior pastors have enjoyed the association with a host of talented and dedicated associates.

Second, shared staff leadership has been the rule. Bethel's program was never dependent and will not depend on a single minister. Each senior pastor surrounded himself with a creative, committed, and loyal pastoral and lay staff. The staff then was freed to work under the guidance of the senior pastor. They were encouraged to create, innovate, and develop outstanding programs without bringing every nuance before the senior pastor for his approval.

However, the pulpit was not filled, nor can it be, by a committee. The senior minister is the principal preacher. Other ordained staff share in the pulpit enough to give them exposure and opportunity to get the support of the congregation for the particular area of responsibility to which they were called.

A thirty-five-year-old mother of three, and a longtime member of Bethel, stressed the importance of the "main preacher" principle. "Bethel has many unique attributes to keep us coming back each Sunday, but the most important one to me has been the quality of the sermons. They are delivered in a way that is both motivating and relevant to my personal life as well as my place in the world. . . . A sense of community and direction surrounds the service, but the cornerstone for me has been the Word and how it has been so adeptly taught from the pulpit."

Third, the staff and volunteer leaders at Bethel have been sensitive to the needs of the community and the world around them.

Fourth, the first-time visitor experiences a warmth and friendliness that is real and meaningful. This congregation is aware that no one can relate to 7,000 people, so Bethel became a congregation of congregations, each addressing clearly defined needs and challenges. It is in these smaller communities where strangers find a home in this large parish.

Fifth, and perhaps most important, this parish has consistently focused on challenges just beyond its reach. We help people grow into what God intended them to be. Likewise, Bethel challenges itself as a parish to reach beyond its grasp.

The leaders are convinced that Bethel has always had a passion for a great adventure, and the leadership of Bethel has not permitted that vision to fade. The gospel is made relevant in warm and personal ways. The social challenges that threaten the common good are never politicized but always put in terms of Scripture and human need. The services as well as the instruction are unabashedly Lutheran in nature. Bethel never became a self-serving experience. Worship is never viewed as an end in itself, but always as a means to an end. Sermon and anthem, hymn and Scripture are blended together in such a way that the Holy Spirit is given a clean shot at those who need to face their own personal crises as well as the crises they encounter in the community around them.

A journalist who returned to Bethel in 1975 after thirteen years out of town summarized the role of Bethel as a university church. "As a church in a university community, Bethel always has filled a role of counterbalancing the secular, scientific skepticism that typifies so many academics. Pastor Bob was particularly gifted in responding to the doubts and challenges shown by the rationalists in our midst. I am concerned that the university is less concerned with these matters today, confronting the ministry with a different, more subtle but perhaps more insidious, form of opponent, one that ignores and dismisses without argument, as though assuming the church is irrelevant and therefore unworthy of discussion. It is harder to argue with silence. But it may be more urgent." Bethel, as a congregation, has remained true, from its very beginning, to Jesus when he said, "If you continue in my word, you are truly my disciples; and you will know the truth, and the truth will make you free" (John 8:32).

Those words are sufficient guidance for any congregation entering the twenty-first century.

14.

A New Immigrant Church

Sang E. Chun

> And the ransomed of the LORD shall return,
>   and come to Zion with singing;
> *everlasting joy* shall be upon their heads;
>   they shall obtain joy and gladness,
> and sorrow and sighing shall flee away.
> (Isa. 35:10, italics added)

On December 2, 1945, a group of twenty-seven Christian refugees from North Korea came together in Seoul, South Korea, for their first worship service.

The membership increased rapidly, and the church was named the Young Nak Prebyterian Church. (*Young Nak* translates into English as "everlasting joy.")

Thirty-nine months after that first worship service, ground was broken for construction of a new stone sanctuary. It was first used for worship on June 4, 1950. A few weeks later the North Korean army swept across the border and drove the

Young Nak members into exile. Their building was seized by the North Korean Communists.

While in exile, the members helped to build new churches in Pusan, Taegu, and on Cheju Island. Finally, four and a half years after they first worshiped in their beautiful new church home, the building was returned to them and was dedicated on December 19, 1954.

When the founding pastor retired in early 1973, the Young Nak congregation included 15,000 communicants. It peaked in size in the mid-1980s with 60,000 members. This evangelistic congregation has sent missionaries to Japan, Nigeria, Chile, Brazil, West Germany, the United States, India, Taiwan, Uganda, and a dozen other countries.

During the 1970s thousands of immigrants from Korea came to the United States. This flow included members of the Young Nak congregation, some of whom settled in Los Angeles. They found three Korean churches already established, but they missed the spirit of their church back home in Seoul. In their search for the everlasting joy they had known in Korea, thirty-nine former members of the Young Nak Church in Seoul and their friends came together for worship on March 4, 1973. They founded the Young Nak Presbyterian Church of Los Angeles. They had no plan, no capital, no pastor, no land, and no outside support.

Later, one charter member reflected on this experience: "Like the early Christians, we enjoyed being together, sharing Korean food, and the fellowship after each worship service."

On their third Sunday they organized a worship committee and a choir. One member of that committee had been a member of the Sao Paulo Korean Church in Brazil, where the Reverend Keyong Kim had been the founding pastor. In less than six years that new mission had grown from 60 to 1,400 members. That was an impressive record for an immigrant church in Brazil! They called him to be their first shepherd.

Fifty-three weeks after that first worship service, Reverend Kim arrived to be greeted by 236 members. They had been meeting in the chapel of the First Presbyterian Church of Hollywood, but they longed for their own place. They needed a place they could use at any hour, where they could cook traditional Korean food and enjoy their fellowship with one another.

Trusting that the Lord would provide, they decided to purchase an old Jewish synagogue located in the northwestern part of Korea-town. The old building had a 900-seat sanctuary, a 200-seat chapel, and a fellowship hall that would accommodate 400. Except for the parking lot, which could hold only thirty cars, the size and location was ideal for this fast growing church, and the congregation moved in on July 8, 1975.

Expanding the Ministry

This new congregation now had a shepherd, their own meeting place, and a model. Their vision was to model this new congregation after the Young Nak Presbyterian Church in Seoul.

As part of their expanding ministry, they purchased a church cemetery in the Rose Hill Memorial Park of Los Angeles and named it Young Nak Rose Garden. Members could now be comforted at the pain and sorrow of burying their loved ones in this strange land far away from their home. The Young Nak family conducts an annual memorial service at the Rose Garden during the *Chusuk,* the full moon in August of the Lunar Calendar, the Korean Thanksgiving Day. It is a long established custom to have these annual memorial services for ancestors and visits to the cemetery during Chusuk season.

One of the most significant changes came in 1978 with the inauguration of a television ministry. The half-hour program "Morning of Hope" first aired on August 20, 1978. During the next two years the membership nearly doubled to 1,497, and 60 percent of the newcomers said they first came after hearing the Reverend Kim's sermons on television. This ministry has grown to include their own recording studio, an $80,000 budget, and a new format under the title "The Hour of Hope."

Korean Christians take the Great Commission of Jesus Christ (Matt. 28:19-20) very seriously. As soon as they grew strong enough to support a new congregation, they began to extend their church into surrounding areas. In 1980 a new congregation, Young Nak Presbyterian Church of Orange County, was sponsored in the El Toro area. In 1981, the Young Nak Presbyterian Church of Lancaster was organized.

Growth Means Change!

Following the tradition of most Korean churches, the Young Nak Church conducts annual revival services that are both spiritually uplifting and supportive of new ministries, such as world missions, serving second-generation young people, and building programs. The May 1983 revival produced pledges of nearly $1.6 million for a new building.

As the congregation outgrew that old Jewish synagogue, they rented space in a high school three miles away. This also provided additional parking.

After a long search, a five-acre parcel in the northern part of Los Angeles was purchased in October 1986, and a year later a $9 million building program was launched. Twenty months later, in their sixteenth year of existence, the Young Nak congregation moved into their 1,700-seat sanctuary. This facility also includes a 500-car parking lot, offices, classrooms, and other meeting rooms. It is somewhat ironic, though, to see the largest Korean American Church located in China town. It illustrates an old joke among immigrants from the Pacific Rim that when the Chinese get together, they build a restaurant, the Japanese build a factory, and Koreans build a church.

The next big change came with the retirement of the Reverend Keyong Kim. His integrity, commitment, and democratic leadership won the respect and admiration of everyone. His preaching, along with the television program and the name, stand out as being among the most influential reasons for the rapid growth of this immigrant congregation.

During the Korean War, Keyong Kim came south from North Korea, leaving his wife behind. Thus the Kims became one of those ten million separated families of Korea. The end of World War II divided Korea into two countries: South Korea, a democratic nation, and North Korea, a communist country. Since then, both visitors and mail from the South could not enter the North and vice versa. Even today, only a few Koreans living overseas are allowed to visit North Korea under the strict control of the North Korean government. For over forty years Keyong Kim lived alone and never remarried. He seldom mentioned his family to anyone, but spoke openly about a plan to visit his home in North Korea after his retirement to see if his wife and children were still alive.

Even though the single life is not easy for a pastor of a large-membership church, he was able to maintain celibacy, and that was yet another reason for people to respect him. His sermons were easy to understand, dealing with in-depth Christian truths. His twenty-five-minute sermons, which were usually based on the four Gospels, always dealt with the victorious Christian life after much suffering. They also appealed to many new immigrants through the weekly "Hour of Hope" television programs in the Los Angeles area. His philosophy of ministry can be summarized in these five admonitions:

1. Love your parishioner.
2. Think positively.
3. Be confident in your ministry.
4. Be patient and generous in dealing with your parishioners.
5. Be diligent and work hard.

After his retirement on August 2, 1990, this exemplary man of God was able to return to North Korea to meet his wife and children, whom he had not seen for approximately forty years because of their separation during the Korean War. When he actually met them, he was so excited, so happy, so emotional, and probably so physically tired that he suffered a heart attack. While he was still visiting his family in North Korea, he died on September 1, 1990, in the presence of his wife and children. He was buried in his homeland, which he had longed to visit. May the eternal peace and joy of God be with him now and forevermore.

The Succession

Like many other very large churches, this congregation planned ahead for the inevitable day when the founding pastor would no longer be the leader and shepherd. Rather than wait for the departure of the senior minister, the Session agreed a better strategy was to build in an intentional period of overlap between the predecessor and the successor. The Reverend Kim had established five guidelines for the selection of his successor. The successor must:

1. Be a Presbyterian minister.
2. Be a minister educated in North America.
3. Have experience as a successful pastoral minister in an immigrant church.
4. Have a pastoral leadership style similar to Kim's.
5. Be in his fifties.

The person who exactly fulfilled all five of those criteria was the Reverend Hee Min Park of Toronto, Canada. He is a Presbyterian, a graduate of Princeton School of Theology, and was the successful pastor of the Korean Church in Toronto, Canada, for fourteen years. He was fifty years of age in 1988. Kim invited Park to Los Angeles to be his associate pastor for six months and to take over the moderatorship. Park accepted the invitation and came to join Kim in the building project in February 1988. Just before his retirement, Kim took a sabbatical leave for three months in order to facilitate a smooth transition for his successor, and Park became the acting moderator during Kim's leave. On October 1, 1989, Park was installed as the second moderator, and Kim became the Moderator Emeritus. They continued to serve as a team until Kim's retirement the following August.

The goal of the new pastor for his first year was discipleship training. His methodology calls for him, as the pastor, to train two disciples for three months. Next, each of those two trains two others, and the process continues until every member has been trained.

The goal for the second year was evangelism. The focus was a "Festival of Jesus Gospel," which called for every member to bring new people to church. As a result, on Sunday, June 30, 1991, 15,000 people came to one of the five (7:00, 9:00, 11:00 A.M. and 1:00 and 3:00 P.M..) worship services. They were welcomed, appreciated, given gifts, challenged to accept Jesus Christ as their Lord and Savior, and encouraged to come back or regularly attend a church near their homes. Fifteen thousand persons accepted Jesus, and 300 of these joined Young Nak church after seven weeks of new-member training. Park conducts the new-member training regularly on Wednesday evenings for seven weeks for each class. He deals with issues of community evangelism during the first half of the new-member training and world missions in the second half. He emphasizes the fact that all members of the Christian church are evangelists and missionaries. Two advantages of having new-member classes regularly by the senior pastor are that newcomers have an opportunity to meet the moderator in person as well as meeting other new friends.

Mobility and the Next Generation

Like other immigrant congregations, the Young Nak Presbyterian Church is faced with two difficult issues. One is the mobility of new immigrants. As they become more comfortable with the American culture and economy, many move to the suburbs. Already large Korean congregations exist in Torrence, Irvine, Glendale, and other suburban communities.

The second issue is what happens as the children of immigrants grow into adulthood. What does that mean for what had been created as an immigrant church?

In order to avoid the mistakes that have been made by other minority immigrant congregations, Young Nak Church is carefully studying the history of other minority churches in America. They know how some of the other ethnic minority churches failed to teach their ethnic heritage to their children and grandchildren. For example, once significant Jewish synagogues, one by one, are being sold to Korean immigrant churches. Why? The second generation is rapidly assimilated into the majority culture, and they turn their backs on the faith of their parents. Naturally, as time goes by, membership of the church declines. To prevent a parallel decline, Korean immigrant churches must help their second, third, and future generations to find their identity as Korean-Americans and keep the faith of their parents as their own. Park knows these facts fully through his past experience in Canada, and he provides Bible classes for all age groups. Bilingual education, language and heritage education, mission education for elementary aged children, evangelism training for youth, and stewardship education for adults are being offered during the first year of the three-year cycle, and the subject areas will rotate the following year by age groups.

Kim's vision for tomorrow includes these seven points:

1. Evangelical faith for all members;
2. Service for immigrants;
3. Planned ministry for second-generation immigrants;
4. World mission;
5. Ministry of the laity through discipleship and small-group training;
6. Ministry to the community;
7. Family ministry.

Today the Young Nak Presbyterian Church of Los Angeles, with 6,000 members, stands out as one of the three largest Korean congregations in North America and averages approximately 3,500 at worship. With the experienced and visionary pastoral leadership of the Reverend Hee Min Park, Young Nak Church seems to be ready to face the twentieth anniversary of the church and the twenty-first century to save dying souls and to help hurting people in and around the city and beyond.

What Can We Learn from This Church?

1. Contrary to what many church leaders assume, downtown Protestant churches in large central cities are alive, healthy, and growing! As long as the church effectively meets the needs of the people, that congregation can have a future in the central city.

2. A good, recognizable name for a church, like Young Nak, is a real asset.

3. Vital sermons touch the hearts of people! Preaching that speaks to the spiritual needs as well as to mental and physical needs motivates people to bring others.

4. Excellent sermons should not be restricted only to the members of one local church but should be shared by multitudes of people through mass media, such as television.

5. The pastor is the key to opening the door for growth. Find the right match, the one who has a good track record.

6. Programs such as Young Nak Rose Garden and a television ministry that meets people's real needs are crucial for church growth.

7. Providing ample space for ministry as the congregation grows is another crucial factor for church growth.

8. It is imperative for a congregation to follow the Great Commission of Jesus Christ (Matt. 28:18-20). Evangelism training for all members and an annual evangelism rally certainly lift up the spirit for vitality and growth. A good old-time revival meeting still works for Korean churches.

9. The successor pastor must have a vision for the continuation of the original vision.

15.

Thirty Recurring Themes

Lyle E. Schaller

One of the reasons for publishing this book is to counter the conventional wisdom that has declared American Protestantism cannot survive in that hostile environment we call the central city.

In recruiting contributors to this book, the problem was not in finding vital, growing, dynamic, vigorous, attractive, and strong churches. The most difficult problem was selecting only fourteen from the hundreds and hundreds of highly qualified candidates. The grass is still green in the ecclesiastical landscape of this nation's large cities.

A second reason is to discover what can be learned by examining the life and ministry of a small sample of these central-city churches.

The most obvious, and perhaps the least surprising, of the many themes that run through these chapters is the crucial role of effective pastoral leadership. It is impossible to overstate the critical importance of effective ministerial leadership. Commitment, character, competence, and vision are far more valuable than academic credentials. It is impossible to overstate the importance of skilled, determined, and dedicated pastoral leadership.

Overlapping that is a second recurring theme. This is the power of that God-inspired vision of a new tomorrow. In several chapters it is clear that God's vision for that church greatly exceeded what the founding pastor either dreamed or hoped could happen. These stories document the fact that God is alive and at work in the world, and that world includes the central cities!

That vision of what God is calling a congregation to be and to do is a far more powerful factor than the age or education or previous experience or personality or pedigree of the pastor. The number-one credential shared by these pastors is a commitment to God's vision.

A third recurring theme is long pastorates. This correlation has been documented in scores of other studies of both urban and suburban churches. The larger the size of the congregation, the more likely that much of the continuity is in the person of the senior minister.

A fourth theme that should be at the heart of every denominational strategy for reaching people in the large central cities is summarized in that old cliché "New churches for new generations." One-half of the fourteen congregations in this book were organized in 1960 or later. The majority of all Protestant congregations in the United States founded before 1960 are reporting a numerical decline.

A fifth recurring theme is the centrality of prayer in the lives of these pastors and their churches. While the perspective of the contributor obviously influences the emphasis given this theme, it comes through repeatedly.

For some readers the number-one valuable insight is spelled out most clearly in the chapters on the New York City congregations, one founded in 1662 and the other in 1989. It also is a theme in the stories from Akron, Denver, Des Moines, Seattle, Madison, Los Angeles, Chicago, and Tucson. Suburbanites will come to the central city to worship, but few residents of the central city will go to the suburbs to attend church. This runs completely counter to many of the proposals of the 1960s for cooperative parishes that would include both center-city and suburban congregations.

For other readers the theme that jumps out from these pages is the centrality of the corporate worship of God. This is true of the most liberal as well as of the most conservative churches represented in this volume. Friendship and kinship ties, habit, guilt, institutional loyalties, and peer pressure can be powerful motivators for going to church in suburbia and in small-town America. The anonymity of the large central city largely nullifies those motivating factors. In these and hundreds of other large center-city churches people come largely because of the power and majesty of that worship experience, those relevant, meaningful, memorable, and challenging sermons, and the excellence of that teaching ministry. One lesson is that far higher quality is required to bring the pilgrim back next Sunday than is needed to motivate the loyal long-term member to return next week.

An eighth theme that comes through most clearly in the case studies of the new churches in New York, Chicago, and Los Angeles, but also can be found in several other chapters, is the erosion of inherited loyalties. This is true not only for the adult children of immigrants from the Pacific Rim, but it also is true for the adult children of American-born Anglos and American-born blacks. This is most highly visible in new evangelical congregations where one's inherited denominational affiliation rarely is even mentioned.

Thousands of rural and small-town churches count on the

continued loyalty of the children, grandchildren, and great-grandchildren of earlier pillars. While most do move away for economic or educational reasons, those who remain in that community tend to follow in their parents' and grandparents' religious traditions. The big exception, of course, is the growing proportion who marry into a different religious tradition. By contrast, the large central-city congregations include relatively few adults who can brag, "I've been going to church here since before I was born."

Contrary to conventional wisdom, it is possible for a center-city church to be both large and liberal. This was one reason for including Plymouth Church in Des Moines, but that theme appears in at least four or five other case studies.

While some will argue this should rank higher than tenth on this list of recurring themes, a significant point is that more than one-half of these congregations either have or are planning to plant or sponsor new missions. This, of course, was a widespread practice back in the 1920s and again in the years after World War II, but in the 1950s several denominations decided it would be best to place the responsibility for new church development in either their regional or national headquarters. As the years rolled by, however, the shortage of funds and the competition of other urgent priorities moved this down to a secondary concern. Once again the large central-city churches are accepting the responsibility for planting new missions. (The history of American Protestantism over the past twelve decades suggests that the greater the success of any effort to centralize church planting in denominational headquarters, the fewer the number of new missions that will be planted.)

Overlapping that church planting issue is another theme that is articulated most clearly in the report on Redeemer

Presbyterian Church in New York, but it also comes through in other reports from Chicago, Oklahoma City, Tucson, Los Angeles, Philadelphia, and other places. What is the best way to gather together a group of people to pioneer the creation of a new congregation? Direct mail advertising? Telemarketing? Visiting door-to-door? In the large center-city church the most effective methodology is networking. Plug into the existing social networks. This is especially effective in reaching young never-married adults. The difference between the views of Paul and Peter on this are lifted up in the Oklahoma City account.

While this next theme appears in only a few of these reports, it has great significance for campus ministries. During the third quarter of this century a number of denominational officials were persuaded that the best approach to campus ministries was to detach them from the ongoing life of traditional worshiping communities. The new vision called for the creation of interdenominational and, occasionally, ecumenical arrangements. These specialized ministries in higher education were largely or sometimes completely separated from the worshiping communities that provided most or all of the required financial support. One of the explanations for these arrangements was that this would be a means of competing with the highly popular parachurch organizations that could be found on the campuses of most large universities. The pastors of those congregations that also were attempting to build a ministry with university students occasionally complained that they not only had to finance their own program, but also had to help subsidize their competition.

For a variety of reasons too lengthy to explore here, the next phase in campus ministries has been to tie them to a larger regional parish located near a university campus. This approach is illustrated by the stories of churches in Seattle and Madison.

One of the most provocative of these recurring themes that has powerful implications for inter-church cooperation is identified most clearly in the Tucson narrative, but it appears in several other accounts as well. The new expression of inter-church cooperation is not through denominations coming together in national, state, or metropolitan councils of churches. That was the theme for the first seven decades of the twentieth century. As we prepare to enter the twenty-first century and a new millennium, the pioneering partners in new ventures in inter-church cooperation are senior pastors and large churches, not regional or national judicatories. These new coalitions of large congregations, such as Churches United for Global Mission, represent the model for a new era in inter-church cooperation.

The evolving role of denominations as regulatory agencies is not compatible with a greater emphasis on church planting nor with inter-church cooperation.

Another of the recurring themes that illustrate the new realities of our contemporary society is the importance of music. The basic generalization is the larger the size of the congregation and/or the younger the members and/or the broader the belief system and/or the weaker the kinship or nationality ties, the more important is music in worship. A few will argue this is more apparent west of the Mississippi River than east of it, but do not push that generalization too far! Chicago and Atlanta are east of the Mississippi River.

For those who are still counting, the fifteenth, and one of the most common, themes is the value of offering people choices. This generalization applies to music, the format or approach to worship, the schedule, the teaching ministries, and the opportunities to be engaged in doing ministry. The central city, like large high schools and cable television, teaches two lessons. The world offers you many choices, but you cannot say yes to all of them.

From the perspective of those responsible for devising a denominational strategy for ministry in the central city, a key theme is independence. As was pointed out in the introduction, the missionary goal of self-governing, self-propagating, and self-supporting has been realized in the best of today's central-city churches. All too often denominational tactics encourage a dependency relationship that is incompatible with the character of the missionary church in the central city.

The big exception to this generalization is in those denominations that place a high priority on a network of small congregations, each staffed with a seminary-trained and full-time resident pastor, scattered across the central city. Implementation of that strategy does require substantial financial subsidies and, of course, does tend to create a dependency relationship. This strategy also illustrates the natural tendency for dependency relationships to evolve into adversarial relationships. That financial subsidy is never as large or as dependable as "fairness" or "justice" requires.

For obvious reasons the contributors to this volume have been reluctant to emphasize another recurring theme. The basic generalization is the higher the density of population, the greater the degree of anonymity in that local culture, the weaker the cohesive power of kinship ties, the younger the age of the people and/or the larger the congregation, the easier it is for people to switch from one congregation to another. Large central-city congregations include three passing parades. One consists of people coming from other congregations. A second consists of new converts and the return of those who had dropped out years earlier. The third consists of people leaving for another church. In the best of the churches the first and second parades include more people than are to be found in that third parade. One of the ways to expand the third is a series of short pastorates.

The notable exception to that opening generalization in the previous paragraph is kinship ties may continue to be reinforced by that anonymity among the first generation of newcomers and sometimes even the second generation of newcomers from a different culture and/or another continent.

Another theme of special significance for both congregational policy makers and denominational leaders is the central city can be a compatible environment for the large regional church. As was pointed out earlier, suburbanites will come into the central city to worship, but central-city residents are far less likely to go to church in suburbia. Two-thirds of the congregations described in this book are regional churches. The descriptions of the ministries of these regional churches underscores the fact that a seven-day-a-week ministry is an essential element in fulfilling the role of a regional church in a large metropolitan area. Many of the congregations described here have followed what has become a classic pattern of evolving from neighborhood or immigrant parishes into community congregations into regional churches. Jesus People USA, described in the third chapter, is the number-one example in this volume of a neighborhood congregation.

This helps to explain why many of the long-established central-city churches have been able to grow younger and larger. They draw from a large area. More important, however, is the fact that in today's society, thanks partly to the return to the churches of those adults born after 1955, growing younger and larger are two highly compatible goals for a central-city church. That theme recurs repeatedly in these pages.

One of the most significant trends in American Christianity during the last third of the twentieth century has been the rediscovery of the third person of the Holy Trinity. For decades most Protestant congregations, regardless of location, focused largely on either the first or second person of the Trinity. While they did not monopolize it, center-city churches led in the rediscovery of the Holy Spirit. This has been most highly visible in those congregations reaching large numbers of adults born after 1945. One of the implications for many center-city churches has been the need for a bigger umbrella to embrace a broader range of theological belief systems. This is a low-key, but important, theme in several chapters.

If this list were to be compressed from thirty into five, this twenty-first theme would have to stand alone as a central characteristic of the missionary church in the central city today. It includes two facets: (1) the rediscovery of what the early Christians called "the seven corporal works of Christian mercy—to feed the hungry, clothe the naked, shelter the homeless, care for the orphan, tend the sick, visit the prisoner, and bury the dead" and (2) challenging the people to volunteer to be engaged in doing ministry. That is a highly visible, recurring theme in these chapters.

The most recent addition to this list of expectations is that central-city churches should create employment opportunities for people. The two dramatic illustrations of this facet of ministry in this volume are Jesus People USA in Chicago (chap. 3) and Deliverance Church in Philadelphia (chap. 5).

Overlapping this is the redefinition of *missions*. Forty years ago a common synonym for *missions* was *overseas*. Today the synonym is *in our own backyard*. One expression of this is a growing proportion of the money designated for missions is allocated locally and a diminishing proportion is poured into denominational pipelines.

A related theme is the higher expectations the public places on the churches in the central city. People place high expectations on these churches. One of these is that the church is a place to turn to for help in solving problems. One result has been that tremendous expansion in Twelve-Step recovery groups. These range from recovery groups for substance abusers to divorce recovery workshops to help for the adult children of alcoholic parents to support for the children who are the victims of a traumatic divorce to the support system for the single parent.

One of the themes that many prefer to avoid is a highly visible trend. Unless a persistent effort is made to buck this trend, women are becoming a larger part of the constituency of central-city churches. In the 1950s the typical large central-city church reported that 52 to 60 percent of the adults present for worship were women. Today that proportion is more likely to run between 60 and 85 percent.

The three big exceptions to that pattern are (1) those congregations that intentionally, systematically, and persistently build in all-male enclaves (such as a men's Bible study class or a male chorus or a male work team); (2) the churches that operate from a belief system that severely limits the role for women; and (3) the very high commitment churches that project high expectations of both women and men.

Many readers will contend that this next theme should be moved from twenty-fifth to second or third on this list if the goal is to rank them by importance. This is the escalating demand for a greater emphasis on the teaching ministry. This also is the most widely publicized facet of ministry in many of today's large and rapidly growing suburban megachurches. The significance and power of the teaching ministry in center-city churches is illustrated in nearly every congregation described in this volume. The power and attractiveness of good teaching begins with the sermon and extends throughout the total program. People do want to learn, and many look to the church as the best place to learn more about the faith and discipleship. One growing response to this demand is the thirty- to fifty-minute, memorable, visual, and meaningful teaching sermon.

From both a theological and a pragmatic perspective, one of the recurring themes in many center-city churches today is the shift from fund raising to stewardship as the way to pay the bills. The basic generalization is the larger the congregation and/or the faster the rate of numerical growth and/or the greater the population density, the greater the emphasis on stewardship and the lower the role of fund-raising events or denominational subsidies.

Many large center-city churches are hurting from one of the most widely ignored trends of the past half century. More space is required today to accommodate the same number of churchgoers than was needed in 1950. The pew designed for eight now feels crowded if it includes more than five worshipers. The Sunday school classroom designed for twenty now is crowded when fifteen are present. The automobile that brought four or five worshipers in 1950 has been replaced by the three vehicles needed to bring five people today. Perhaps the most common theme in today's center-city churches is "We need more room!"

For many, one of the most regrettable trends of the past half century has been the shift in American society from a strong child orientation in the 1950s to the adult orientation of the 1990s. This adult orientation has become a common characteristic of most churches, both central-city and suburban, but it tends to be stronger in the larger central cities. It is reflected in both public and private priorities. One product of that trend is that the central city has become an increasingly barren and hostile environment for rearing children. A second is the growing proportion of parents employed in center-city school systems who enroll their children in a private school. A third is the growing number of center-city churches that operate a private Christian day school. A fourth is the expansion of weekday ministries in center-city churches for young children, and especially for those who cannot adjust to the values, priorities, and routines of the public schools. The most difficult is to build a ministry with the one in nine center-city children who do not live with either parent. More and more center-city churches are placing a high priority on creating a supportive environment for the family.

It is difficult to overstate the impact of television on the churches in general, but especially on urban congregations. For a growing number of congregations, including a couple in this volume, television has become the most effective single channel for inviting people to that church. Television also has taught people to expect a faster pace in life. That is reflected in the pace of worship in most large central-city churches where worship is an experience, not a passive noun. That theme appears repeatedly in this volume. Television also has changed people's expectations of church in regard to music, the use of color, and a greater emphasis on visual communication, including drama and dance. Television also is making obsolete the linear approach to worship that was reinforced by the typographical era that gradually came to an end in the second half of the twentieth century.

(By offering the reader a linear listing of thirty recurring themes, this writer is assuming that a few other survivors from the typographical age are still reading books. We may be a dying breed, but we're not surrendering without a struggle!)

Finally, one of the most significant themes illustrated by these fourteen congregations is that the ecclesiastical scene in the central city today reflects an unprecedented degree of diversity! As recently as 1950 Roman Catholic, Jewish, Lutheran, Methodist, Presbyterian, Reformed, Congregational, Christian (Disciples of Christ), Southern Baptist, American Baptist, Episcopalian, and a half-dozen black denominations dominated the church scene in the large central cities.

Six of the fourteen congregations in this book do not represent any of the large Protestant denominations that dominated the urban church scene in 1950—and the eight out of fourteen that do sharply overrepresent those traditions. The mosaic is both more complex and more colorful than it was in 1950.

So What?

While not offered as a comprehensive summary of the characteristics of Protestant ministries in the central cities, these thirty themes do illustrate three points.

First, life is complicated! Doing ministry in the large central city may be fun, but it is neither simple nor easy. It is challenging, and meeting challenges can produce immense satisfaction, but that effort also can result in a string of frustrating experiences.

Second, these thirty themes are offered for those who seek a conceptual framework for analyzing their own situation. Which of these themes is relevant to how you do ministry in the place God has called you to be and to fill? What are the implications?

Third, these themes also can be used in creating that conceptual framework required to design a relevant and effective denominational strategy for ministry in large central cities. Instead of seeking to recreate 1954, it may be wiser to recognize that the urban frontier of today is not an older version of 1954.

A Denominational Strategy

What is the strategy of your denomination for the central cities of America? In a few cases a comprehensive strategy has been thoughtfully and carefully articulated. In most traditions, however, the operational strategy can be perceived only by looking at a series of separate decisions.

One operational strategy is to gradually reduce the number of congregations via mergers and closures.

Another is based on the goal of maintaining a "denominational presence" through a network of shrinking congregations, nonparochial ministries, and social welfare programs such as anti-drug efforts.

A third is to rely on a series of anchor points built around the combination of a worshiping community and a Christian day school.

A fourth is to look to the television ministry of one congregation to blanket the entire metropolitan area with the weekly proclamation of the good news that Jesus Christ is Lord and Savior.

Perhaps the most promising denominational strategy begins with a simple assumption that is illustrated by the majority of the case studies in this book. The most effective means of reaching new generations of people with the gospel is through new congregations. Whether these new adults be American-born or foreign-born, the most productive component of the strategy for reaching them is new churches for new generations.

The simplest statistical documentation for this priority comes out of the historical record. As a group, the congregations organized in any decade before 1960 (1970 in the case of the Presbyterian Church [U.S.A.]) now report a combined net loss in membership. That same pattern has been reported by Lutherans, Methodists, and others.

The second component of a promising denominational strategy, and some will argue this should be first, is to enlist, train, place, and challenge a large number of talented, competent, creative, productive, committed, and visionary pastors for ministry in the central city. Once again all the churches described in this book support the central importance of competent ministerial leadership. In many of the aging mainline Protestant denominations, this strategy will require substantial changes in the methods and criteria for enlisting, training, and placing the next generation of pastors.

Which denominations will dominate the Protestant scene in urban America in the year 2025? The answer is those that were most successful in attracting the best and the brightest of the babies born in the 1970s and 1980s into choosing the pastoral ministry as their vocation.

Overlapping this is the third component. This is a systematic and intentional effort to create large congregations. The central cities of the pre–World War II era were dominated by small institutions. That list included banks, grocery stores, neighborhood churches, motion picture theaters, savings and loan associations, hardware stores, gasoline stations, hospitals, drugstores, legal services, new car dealers, and the public schools.

There continues to be a place for those small institutions that focus on the individual. These include the small elite private elementary school, the solo lawyer in private practice, the small "Mom and Pop" convenience grocery store, the solitary dentist, and the bridal shop. There also will continue to be a place for the small worshiping community that has carved out a narrowly and precisely defined niche for itself. Eighty percent of the Protestant churchgoers in the central cities of 2025, however, will be worshiping in large congregations. One-fourth or one-fifth of the resources available for implementing that denominational strategy should be allocated to perpetuating small congregations and the rest to the creation of more large congregations.

The fourth component of a productive denominational strategy will be providing the resources and consultation services necessary to help long-established congregations define and implement the changes required to reach and serve new generations of central-city residents. This is a challenging assignment! The best results will be seen in those congregations blessed with a pastor who displays the skills of a transformational leader.

One of the most subtle themes running through most of the chapters in this book can be summarized by a spectrum. This spectrum is defined by the words *autonomy* at one end and *dependency* at the other end. (That same spectrum also can be used to describe a variety of approaches to the rearing of children. In that case it is summarized by the old cliché, "We either give our children wings or we give them roots.")

With only a couple of exceptions, and both are debatable, the churches described in this book are located at or near the autonomy end of that spectrum. Three do not carry a traditional denominational label, and at least six others carry it very lightly.

This introduces the fifth and, for some readers, perhaps the most disturbing factor in the formulation of a denominational strategy. From a denominational value system perspective, do we encourage autonomy or dependency?

It is almost a cliché in today's world that a common characteristic of high-performance organizations is autonomy. This can be seen in education, parachurch organizations, industry, publishing, and megachurches. Autonomy rests on independence, performance, merit, identity, and community. The price tag in contemporary American Protestantism for those five characteristics is a minimal tie with or dependency on a denominational system. For some, including this writer, who are dyed-in-the-wool denominationalists, that can be interpreted as bad news. The natural response is to kill the messenger who bears the bad news. A second is denial, but denial is never a source of hope or creativity.

A more productive response consists of two questions. First, is that true? This observer's experience suggests that autonomy is a characteristic of today's high-performance organizations, including most high-performance churches.

Second, if that is true, how can denominational structures, which often nurture dependency, be reformed to nurture autonomy? One road to answering that question may be in studying the evolution of that new organization called Churches United in Global Mission. To a significant degree this is modeled on the Articles of Confederation adopted by the colonies in 1777–78. By contrast, the Roman Catholic Church, The United Methodist Church, the Episcopal Church, and, to a lesser degree, the Presbyterian Church (U.S.A.) and the new Evangelical Lutheran Church in America have chosen a polity that parallels the United States Constitution with far greater centralized authority.

The Civil War, the New Deal, and the civil rights movement of the 1960s were seen by many historians as events that settled the dispute between states' rights and the authority of the national government. Presidents Ronald Reagan and George Bush and the opponents of huge federal deficits have wanted to reopen that debate.

The temptation is to transfer ideological arguments for civil government to ecclesiastical organizations. That reinforces the notion that the evolution of denominations from agencies designed to facilitate worldwide missions and to service congregations into regulatory agencies is both predictable and good.

In another setting I have attempted to explain that one product of this evolving role of denominations has opened the door for other organizations to service congregations and to mobilize resources for world missions. (See *The Seven-Day-A-Week Church* [Nashville: Abingdon Press, 1992], pp. 17-36.)

Thus it could be argued that perhaps the initial step in articulating a denominational strategy for the central city is not to review the thirty recurring themes in this chapter. Perhaps that first step should be to (1) redefine the reasons for the existence of that denomination, (2) rethink the assumptions about the relationships between the denomination and various types of congregations, (3) examine the available resources for an improvement in the quality of congregational life, (4) agree on assumptions about ministry in today's large central cities, and (5) formulate a set of operational goals that are consistent with the role of that denomination and with those two sets of assumptions.

While that process is taking place, additional new congregations will be organized in the large central city by the newer denominations, by individual entrepreneurs, and by newcomers from other lands to these ports of entry. Meanwhile, every day a couple of central-city congregations will conclude that faithfulness and obedience are not sufficient for institutional survival and will decide to close or to merge into another church. The central city demands performance of the church as well as faithfulness and obedience. Which will be the higher priority in the strategy of your denomination—coming to the aid of the dying or giving birth to the new?